"A powerful book that hits home with millions of us Americans."

"President Trump these past few years has helped millions of people get jobs. He cares for people of all races and is a true American. He fought for the better of our country, and his contribution really made America great again."

"A must-read. Nathan illustrates not only how our country became divided but how the career politicians in Washington, DC, continued to attempt the dismantling of the presidency of Donald J. Trump from the very beginning."

"Nathan takes you through his political-education journey and how it has impacted him and his family along with how the mainstream media has impacted the political geography of the country over the past five years. It's a must-read."

One Term:
A Current-Day Political Assassination

by Nathan Aguinaga

ISBN 978-1-64663-492-7

Published by

köehlerbooks™

3705 Shore Drive
Virginia Beach, VA 23455
800-435-4811
www.koehlerbooks.com

ONE TERM

A CURRENT-DAY
POLITICAL ASSASSINATION

NATHAN AGUINAGA

VIRGINIA BEACH
CAPE CHARLES

Dedicated to the memory of Rush Limbaugh.
Without your voice, this book would not be possible.
Thank you for paving the way for conservative commentary.

TABLE OF CONTENTS

Whoever controls the present controls the past. To wipe away history means one will never learn from it; this is the concept of George Orwell's book *1984*, published in 1949.

In my personal opinion, the top five presidents in the history of the United States are in this order: one, George Washington, one of our Founding Fathers and the first president of our nation; two: Abraham Lincoln, who rid our nation of slavery; three, Ronald Reagan, who defeated the Soviet Union and won the Cold War against communism; four, Donald J. Trump, who brought our nation back as the economic and military superpower of the world within three years of a first-term presidency; five, John F. Kennedy, who stood up and threatened nuclear war with the Soviet Union at the height of the Cold War in order to prevent their nuclear dominance in the Western Hemisphere. In today's political world of 2021, he would be considered a moderate Republican.

NATHAN AGUINAGA,
Retired US Army and Author

FOREWORD

I grew up in a small town, technically a village, in Northern Ohio that had more Catholic churches than stoplights. Most of my peers had parents and grandparents that grew up in the same small town, and we were all cut from basically the same cloth. When I turned eighteen in the early part of my senior year of high school, I was excited to vote in the 2000 Bush/Gore election. I proudly cast my Republican vote and have in every election since.

After college and getting married, my husband and I left Ohio and moved to the DC metro area to start our married lives and careers. Within a month of newlywed bliss, my husband received his alert orders for his first deployment to go overseas to Kuwait and Iraq. My Republican views were no longer those of my family or community; they were truly my own.

It was 2008, and my husband was conducting convoy security in Iraq. The defense budget or potential cuts to it were my absolute number one political priority. After Obama won the election, a then coworker asked if I was happy Obama won because "he was going to bring all the troops home!" I looked at her and said, "Not only is he not bringing the troops home, but Democrats also cut the defense budget so they won't have proper equipment. No, I'm not happy Obama won." Our relationship was never the same.

Years later, about ten years after living in the DC area, the political climate had really changed, Trump was president, and the Republicans were still very much the "silent majority." I was out to lunch with two of my closet friends from work, women I had known for almost a decade, when Pete Buttigieg came up in conversation. One friend asked if I was a Buttigieg fan, and I just blurted out, "No, I'm a Republican!" These are women that knew my life, knew I am a practicing Catholic, and knew my combat-veteran husband. These women were my friends. Their faces twisted up and their mouths literally gaped open upon hearing one of their friends proclaim they were a Republican. They questioned me; they poked and prodded into my beliefs. They were disgusted that I was a Republican and Trump supporter. Again, our relationships have never been the same.

I am proud to have known Nate for almost fifteen years, and he is a dear friend. I love his stories, his fun spirit, and his love and commitment to his family. Nate's newest book, *One Term*, is exactly what America needs to hear right now. Nate investigates some of the most powerful current events that our country has faced in recent history. He also explains his personal divide that affects him to this day. I know you will enjoy this book and hearing of Nate's personal experience with politics and his own motivations for making America great again.

—LISA YEARSIN FLORES,
Support Contactor to the Office
of Naval Research

INTRODUCTION

Make no mistake about it. I am not a politician, nor do I ever aspire to be one. I am a retired military guy living in Middle America, in a small farm town in Northwest Ohio named North Baltimore, just south of Toledo. Trust me when I say most of the people in this area of the United States feel the same way I do. By that I mean that we all pretty much share the same concerns and values of everyday life: working, supporting our families, and raising our children to be more successful than us. I would estimate that about 95 percent of this community is Republican and, furthermore, are solid Trump supporters.

Yes, we are the "forgotten people of Middle America." We are the "losers who shop at Walmart." As President Barrack Obama once elegantly put it, we "cling to our guns and our religion." We are the "deplorables" that Hillary Clinton warned you of. We are the sixty-three million Americans that voted for President Trump in 2016, and the over seventy-four million that voted for him for a second term in 2020.

Welcome to my fourth book, ladies and gentlemen! These are stories of my personal beliefs and opinions on why and how I became a Trump supporter. In this book I will explain to you why I changed from being a Democrat supporter to a Republican one, and how that affected my relationship with friends and family. I will tell you how myself and most of "Middle America" feel about this tragic loss during the 2020 election and about our fear of the Democrats taking over the White House, the House of Representatives, and the Senate.

This book will interest, educate, and entertain you, and explain why I am who I am when it comes to being a Donald J. Trump supporter in today's world. Trust me, if you are friends with me on Facebook, you already know my beliefs. Hell, I have lost family and friends over it. I'll get into more details throughout this book. Unfortunately, this loss has been repeated in a lot of relationships throughout our nation over the past several years. We are a divided country for sure. I'm on the side of the GOP but more so the American blue-collared worker.

Did these divisions begin with Trump entering politics, or did they exist decades before him? I will illustrate my opinions about that during the following chapters.

CHAPTER 1

FROM DEMOCRAT
TO REPUBLICAN

The first president I ever voted for was Bill Clinton, back when I was a twenty-year-old soldier. I sent an absentee ballot because I was stationed in Germany at the time but was a resident of the state of Michigan. This is the legitimate mail-in-ballot procedure: You request a ballot from the state of your home of record. They in turn mail you a request form for verification of your signature, date of birth, and social security number. Your signature is then verified on the actual ballot from the request form, which is a pretty secured and verified system of voting. Most military personnel have to use this method; allowing those stationed or working away from their home of record to vote is the main purpose of an absentee ballot.

Anyway, I was born and raised in the "thumb area" of Michigan, in a small city named Lapeer. Lapeer was basically a town of blue-collared workers under the unions, mostly United Auto Workers. A lot of the employment was down in Detroit and nearby Flint, at the massive auto plants. Lapeer is approximately sixty miles north of Detroit and sixteen miles east of Flint. Most of my friends' dads worked for General Motors, Ford, or Chrysler. Many autoworkers lived up north in our area because, to be honest with you, nobody wanted to live in the crime-filled environments of Detroit and Flint. I'm talking in the late seventies and early eighties.

So, pretty much all of these union workers—including my father, who had worked and retired from the state of Michigan's Department of Mental Health—were Democrat supporters. That's the way most of us grew up in that town, back in those days. I remember asking my dad about the difference between Republican and Democrat when I was a little boy during the Reagan and Carter presidential race in 1980. His response was simple: "Republicans are for the rich, and Democrats take care of the poor and lower income." I was sold; it made perfect sense to my eight-year-old self. We didn't have a lot of money, and my dad worked two jobs. He worked at the Lapeer State Home known as Oakdale Center, which housed mentally handicapped adults and even children and was also a foster care facility in the 1930s and 1940s. This facility was one of the largest mental health facilities in Michigan.

My father would come home around three o'clock in the afternoon, eat, and then take a few-hours nap, get up, shower, get ready, and go play in a band at a nightclub. He was and still is an excellent drummer and a great singer. In the '70s and '80s, live bands were the main source of entertainment in most dance clubs. When the bars closed at one or two in the morning, he would drive home, usually from a big club in the Detroit area or, later on, clubs in Flint. Then he would turn around and get up at five and go to his day job.

He did that shit throughout my entire childhood. My mom was a stay-at-home mom, and for the longest time she would babysit the neighborhood kids, get us all off to school, and be there when we got off the bus in the afternoon. The bottom line is that we always had a solid income because my parents worked their asses off constantly. We weren't rich by any means, but who was back in those days? We never went without—that I can tell you.

Anyhow, due to the mentality of that era, most people in that area voted for and supported the Democrats as "the party of the unions." Although my parents and most of my family on both sides continue to be Democrat supporters today, I believe my parents both voted for Ronald Reagan in 1980 over Jimmie Carter. Let's face it, plenty of Democrats voted for Reagan coming out of the 1970s. Look how the '70s turned out for the United States from the world's view, especially our foreign affairs and relationships with other nations: We were in the height of the Cold War with the Soviet Union. We were just coming out of the Vietnam conflict in an embarrassed withdrawal and defeat, which resulted in pretty much all of Southeast Asia becoming a communist region. This included the genocidal, murderous regime of the Khmer Rouge in Cambodia.

Next, in the Watergate scandal, Nixon's administration was caught spying on his opponent's campaign during the election year for his second-term attempt. Instead of fighting the House of Representatives on his inevitable impeachment proceedings, he simply resigned before the American people, live from the Oval Office. Vice President Gerald Ford took over as the thirty-eighth president and finished out the rest of Nixon's term.

Then we had Carter, whose first-term administration, in my opinion (and this entire book is opinionated), went down as one of the biggest failures in US history. If the United States wasn't already labeled as a weak nation by our adversaries across the globe by then, what ensued during Carter's presidency cemented that impression. Islamic extremist groups were introduced to the world, and especially to the United States. The Iran hostage crisis, which lasted over 400 days, was the icing on the cake for Carter's failed presidency—the first administration that I remember as a young child.

Reagan gave our country, both Republicans and Democrats, hope for the United States' comeback as a global superpower. He won in a landslide against President Carter. He has gone down in history as the president that defeated the Soviet Union and brought them to economic collapse.

In college, I had a history professor who explained the economic "squeeze" that President Reagan achieved, all due to the nonexistent

Star Wars program. This professor called it the biggest bluff any nation had made to a major adversary in history. To this day, we do not have the technological capability to shoot lasers from outer space into our hemisphere in order to destroy a rocket. However, according to history, the Soviet Union bought it. Every time President Reagan attended a summit with Russian leadership, they attempted to negotiate with him to slow down our progress or simply dissolve the Star Wars program. Reagan in turn would deny their request, and furthermore had them convinced that we had almost completed the project. Russia poured more money into their defense and military, trying to outdo the United States, and eventually their economy collapsed. It was a brilliant, bold, and brave move on the Reagan administration's part. Soviet-controlled nations in Eastern Europe such as East Germany, Poland, Romania, and Yugoslavia, to name just a few, regained their statuses as sovereign nations. Everyone remembers Reagan's speech in West Berlin where he commanded, "Mr. Gorbachev, tear down this wall!" "Peace through strength" was his motto.

I voted for Bill Clinton in 1992, thinking he would be a strong president for our nation, and for the most part (in my opinion) he was. I was on one of the sixty or seventy aircraft headed to Haiti in 1994 when I first got assigned to the 82nd Airborne Division. President Clinton had ordered the launch of the largest airborne invasion since World War II, against a communist military coup that temporarily took over the government of Haiti.

We stayed on Pope Air Force Base, our launch point for Fort Bragg, for almost an entire week, waiting for the weather to clear during the heart of hurricane season. President Clinton had already given the "green light" for us to invade. All three brigades (at the time) from the 82nd Airborne Division would parachute assault on two separate drop zones in Haiti. I was supposed to drop on "Pegasus," on the outskirts of Port-au-Prince. It was going to be my sixth jump, having just arrived to the 82nd, and trust me when I say my ass was puckered tight. My "cherry blast," or first jump since Airborne School, was going to be in combat. We were briefed by intelligence that our drop zone was layered with metal containers that had metal spikes welded to the tops of them. Yeah, we were pretty fucking scared.

About an hour out from drop time, we were ordered to turn around in midair. The communist coup stood down after their leadership found out that the entire 82nd Airborne Division, plus Marines, plus special operation forces, were on our way for a full-blown United States military invasion. The jumpmaster of our C-130 aircraft held up a sign that read, *Heading back to Bragg.*

I respected President Clinton for having the balls to initiate such a mission but at the same time was relieved of the fear that we all had on those airplanes, knowing that we were going to take massive casualties. Fuck it, we were willing to do it either way; we were the 82nd Airborne, and that's what we do. I respected President Clinton as I did John F. Kennedy for having the fortitude to confront and threaten the Soviet Union with nuclear war if they did not remove their ships delivering nuclear weapons to our hemisphere during the Cuban Missile Crisis. Of course, that was about ten years before my time.

During the Monica Lewinski scandal towards the end of Clinton's second term, I never even cared. I was realistic about it: Who cared about him having an affair and his sex life, as long as he continued to run our country in a positive manner? As a matter of fact, me and my fellow soldiers would high-five each other and give him props for someone his age getting a blow job and/or getting laid by a twenty-year-old intern in the Oval Office of the White House. You have to understand young infantrymen's mentality. Hell, JFK used to have affairs in the White House, and even had his Secret Service agents watch out for him while he was with these women. This included skinny-dipping in the White House's indoor pool room. And he was one of the most beloved presidents in American history.

Now let's fast-forward a couple years to the tragedy of September 11, 2001. Within his first seven months of being the forty-third president of the United States, President George W. Bush became a wartime president without wanting or asking for it. He was supposed to be the peacetime president for education reform, but on September 11, 2001, the world fundamentally changed forever—or at least for our lifetime. We were in a new war against an ideology that will continue to exist into our grandchildren's lifetime. I truly believe that.

I was a drill sergeant at the time, only a year into my duty. I had at least another year before I could get back to the 82nd Airborne and get into this new war. I and other drill sergeants were hungry for it, and pissed off that we were "locked into" the world of TRADOC (the Army's Training and Doctrine Command). We wanted to get back into the real Army and go fight these motherfuckers. That was our mentality. Especially those of us who came from the combat arms environment in the military. I go into more detail of this in my last book, *Wake Up, You're Having Another Nightmare.*

I'll never forget how unified our nation was after the 9/11 attacks. Our entire country was "hungry" for revenge on Al Qaeda. This was our generation's Pearl Harbor. We had been attacked on our own soil, and there would be hell to pay for it. I clearly remember President Bush warning the entire world, "You're either with us or against us." He also warned that the United States was going on the offense against all adversaries across the globe. However, the first stop was Afghanistan, the nucleus of Al Qaeda and the Taliban, which harbored Al Qaeda leadership and cells.

Eventually, I finished my time as a drill sergeant, went back to the 82nd, and after some training (which I talk about in my previous books), deployed to Iraq with my battalion. My unit had just returned from their first deployment to Afghanistan when I arrived from my duties as a drill sergeant, so I missed that show.

Why go into Iraq? "Iraq didn't attack us on 9/11" seemed to be a major argument when we started sending thousands of troops over there. I have a simple answer, the same I've had for the past seventeen years: "You are either with us or against us." Remember that comment from the former president?

I watched live on CNN (yes, I used to watch CNN on a regular basis) as the president of Iraq, Saddam Hussein, picked up a silver-plated .45-caliber pistol and fired it in the air to celebrate 9/11. I knew then that Iraq would be next. After Operation Desert Storm, which I was part of as well, Saddam tested the United States on a regular basis, continuously flying over the no-fly zones established after his defeat in 1991 by the US and Coalition Forces.

Many people do not know this, but from 1993 to 2000, under the Clinton administration, the United States would drop bombs on facilities across Iraq for violations of the treaty they signed, including flying over no-fly zones and continuously not allowing United Nation inspectors to inspect their chemical facilities. The US probably conducted air attacks on Iraq at least once a month. Like General Norman Schwarzkopf warned General Powell and President George H. W. Bush in 1991, "If we don't go after the Saddam Hussein regime now, we'll be back over there within ten years." It was actually twelve years, but he was spot on and was told to retire after that.

God forbid career politicians take the word of a seasoned and experienced general officer, right? The situation was similar to President Obama's decision in 2011 to withdraw from Iraq. US commanders in Iraq continuously advised him to leave at least six to seven thousand troops—about the equivalent of two brigade combat teams—in the region in the event another terrorist organization arrived in the area, such as ISIS. Obama and Biden refused, and ordered a 100 percent withdrawal of all US forces. How did that turn out? Two years later, ISIS controlled the majority of Syria and half of Iraq. A year after that, they were conducting attacks throughout Europe and Northern Africa.

Okay, going back to 2004 when I got home from Iraq and my second combat deployment to the Middle East, our units demobilized for a couple weeks, and then we were sent home for a well-deserved fourteen-day block leave. When I arrived in Michigan, I received plenty of hugs and kisses. I also received a lot of "we're so glad you are home in one piece and safe." What I did not receive was any "congratulations on a job well done." Not that I wanted to talk about my experiences over there, but there were also no questions or conversations about my daily life in Iraq this go-round, unlike when I returned home at age nineteen from Desert Storm in '91. Back then it was more of a hero's welcome. In 2004, I got the vibe from family members that they were not as supportive of Operation Iraqi Freedom as they were for Operation Desert Storm thirteen years prior. I mean, they even had Desert Storm sweatshirts and the yellow ribbons, etc. Not this time. I started to see the turn-away mentality concerning the Global War on Terrorism, especially when it came to fighting in Iraq.

As I sat at my parents' kitchen table for dinner one evening when I came home to visit, my father asked me if I had ever killed anyone in Iraq. I answered him honestly, and he simply shook his head. At the time, I didn't know whether he was disappointed in me. I didn't dwell on it too much. After all, my mom was making homemade Mexican food, which I hadn't eaten in over a year.

My brother eventually arrived for dinner as well. He gave me a hug, and we sat down and began catching up with the current events of our lives. He was in college at Western Michigan University. My parents and brother had moved from Lapeer to the Kalamazoo area when I was a young soldier, years before, after the state of Michigan closed down the mental health facility that my father worked at for twenty years. He was hired at the Kalamazoo Psychiatric Hospital. They still live there, in the same home that they bought nearly thirty years ago. My dad eventually retired a few years ago. That area of Michigan is definitely a Democrat stronghold.

Eventually my brother and I got into discussions about the Iraq War. He immediately disagreed with our presence in that particular region. I came back at him with my total dissent. I, a platoon sergeant who had just spent his second tour in that region, found myself arguing with a brother who is ten years younger than me and was in college. He actually tried to educate me on why our presence in that country was wrong. I then realized I was arguing with someone who had been indoctrinated by the education system of that area of Michigan.

When my parents moved to the Kalamazoo area, I believe my brother was in the fifth or sixth grade. I was still a young soldier, recently graduated from Army Airborne School. I gave my little brother my original jump wings that had been punched into my chest during graduation. I wanted him to have them. My mom later sent me his school picture where he was proudly wearing them on his sweater. I think I still have that picture of him. I used to display it in my barracks room at Fort Bragg. The time period was around 1994.

Let's fast-forward a few years to when he was in high school. I came home on leave and took my parents and brother to the movie theater in Portage to see *Saving Private Ryan*. I had already seen it at least twice already at Fort Bragg. I don't need to tell you how phenomenal and powerful the movie is, especially when you have a family member that served in World War II, such as our grandfather.

When the movie was over, the entire theater was silent, as it had been the first two times I saw it. When we got into the parking lot, I asked the family what they thought of the movie. My parents seemed amazed by it, but my brother was not. As a matter of fact, he went off on a rant about how he was disgusted with the United States' involvement in Europe during WWII. I asked him what his problem was, and his response was, "The Germans did not attack us at Pearl Harbor; the Japanese did! Therefore, we had no reason whatsoever to be involved in the European portion of the war."

I reminded him that our grandfather fought in WWII, and then I asked where he was getting this mentality. My father said that they taught them this in school. I sat silently on the ride home, a little bothered, but didn't say anything, and simply let it go. I didn't really think too much of it. Hell, I was only in my early twenties, living in the barracks, busting my young ass in the Army, and partying on the weekends with my friends. That was my entire life. What did I care what my teenage brother thought about US involvement in WWII?

Now fast-forward again, and my brother wants to argue with me at our parents' kitchen table about US involvement in Iraq during the Global War on Terrorism. You can imagine what was going on in my head, having just gotten home from that lethal environment. I was convinced that the liberal, progressive school system had indoctrinated him into their ideology. Today he is a high school principal in the same school district.

Around 2005 I noticed that the country as a whole was turning its back against the war in Iraq, especially once the American death count started escalating. It got worse after the Abu Ghraib prison incident; all service members over there were utterly embarrassed by how a few fucking idiots conducted themselves. Also, it didn't help that there were no weapons of mass destruction found yet—another ongoing argument from the left. My response to all those on the left who wish to argue that point, back then and even now, is simple. Yes, they did.

It is proven in history. Saddam Hussein launched biological/chemical weapons at Iranians during the eight-year-long Iraq–Iran War and also used them on his own people in the northern Iraq sector, against the Kurdish population. That's why I spent almost the entire time during Operation Desert Storm in full chemical gear—because they had SCUD missiles with chemical warheads that they would launch randomly at Coalition Forces in the middle of the desert. So, nobody's going to convince me or those who served in Desert Storm that Saddam didn't have them.

I and many others believe that shit was sold off and shipped up north to Syria. Hell, President Bush gave them over two months' warning that we were going to invade if he and his sons did not stand down from power. You don't think Saddam could have ordered the Iraqi Army to get rid of them in that time? Either way, Saddam Hussein and his two sons were taken out. Saddam was captured by US forces in 2003 and three years later was put to death by the new

Iraqi government for crimes against humanity. He was hung at Camp Justice in northwest Baghdad, where I got deployed a couple years afterward for thirteen months.

Me at age eighteen in northern Saudi Arabia. Operation Desert Storm—1991. I was eight months out of high school, and I had to grow up really fast. This was when I realized that it's our teenagers who fight our wars. God bless them.

In 2006, at the height of the war in Iraq, the United States was losing at least a hundred service members per month, with over a hundred more severely wounded. Our country was understandably losing patience with this war. Lack of concern about a winning outcome grew by the day, and signs of complete withdrawal emerged in Washington, DC. By this time, I realized that CNN, ABC, NBC, and CBS were only covering the negative aspects of this conflict. None of the wins were being reported by these so-called journalists, reminding me of the constant negative coverage of Vietnam. The war in Afghanistan was barely even acknowledged; all attention was directed toward the massive number of deaths and casualties in Iraq, and the negative coverage of President Bush. I mean, they were tearing this man down every hour on the hour. That's a fact.

This was when I began watching the Fox News Channel, and I've been with them ever since. If you are friends with me on social media, you know this.

Anyway, around mid to late 2004, I made up my mind to become a registered Republican. I witnessed the country shift away from the strong support we showed for our country's leadership after the horrific attacks of September 11, 2001. In a state of panic and despair, we all came together. Then sacrifice became the norm in fighting against these Islamic extremists in the Middle East after a couple of years. Yes, this is what happens in war, people. Just ask the WWII, Korean, Vietnam, Grenada, Panama, Desert Storm, Somalia, and Kosovo veterans— they'll tell you all about it.

Iraq was no different, other than a new political concept being pushed by these career politicians: nation building. No sir, it does not work that way, especially in the Middle East. Shiite and Sunni Muslims have been fighting for literally thousands of years over their ideologies. Western Christians will never get into their way—ever. Yes, we will defeat them militarily, as we did consistently in Desert Storm and the Global War on Terrorism, but we will never change their ideology or their hatred of our ideology.

That was the problem with Bush's strategy in that war; he listened to ex-military admirals and generals turned career politicians, such as John McCain and Colin Powell: "You need to have an exit strategy in Iraq and Afghanistan, Mr. President." Thousands of service members have paid the price for this nation-building concept. Many friends and family would tell me, "Yeah, but they're Republicans, Nate." Welcome to the deep state of the Washington, DC, swamp, my friends. I'll get into that in more detail a little bit later. Do you see where I'm going with this book?

Let's fast-forward again to the 2008 presidential race between Senator Barrack Obama and Senator John McCain. Don't forget,

McCain was a retired admiral from the US Navy, and a naval pilot during the Vietnam conflict. He had been shot down over enemy territory and captured. He spent five years in a North Vietnamese prison, famously known as the Hanoi Hilton. John McCain was regularly tortured, and had both his arms and shoulders broken several times. He was even given the option for early release because his father was a famous admiral. When he refused due to others being there longer than him, he was tortured again, almost to the point of death. This was a tough son of a bitch, a hero, and a true *Rambo* story. He was finally released from the Hanoi Hilton along with his 108 captured comrades in 1973, during the US withdrawal from Southeast Asia.

After retiring as an admiral, he began a life into politics. By the time he ran for president of the United States, he was close to being a thirty-year politician, with two terms as Arizona's first district congressman, and twenty-two years as a US senator from Arizona before he ran and was selected as the primary Republican candidate for the 2008 presidential election. It is safe to say that at this point, he was a career politician.

How was Barrack Obama, a one-term US senator from Illinois, able to defeat a career politician and decorated prisoner-of-war veteran? Of course, like I said in the beginning of this book, this is my opinion and the opinion of many in Middle America, but I see two main reasons. First, let's not sugarcoat it: the last term of the Bush administration was not the most popular with the American voter. We had the housing market collapse, which drove our nation into an economic recession. At the same time, the Global War on Terrorism cost trillions of dollars and we were losing thousands of Americans. And we still never came up with weapons of mass destruction in Iraq. CNN, MSNBC, ABC, CBS, and pretty much every other media network were not helping either.

The Republicans in Washington, DC, were not looking so good to the average American voter. As a matter of fact, I remember President Bush saying on national news that he would only endorse

Senator McCain if he specifically asked him to. That is not normal politics for these guys. When have you ever witnessed a leaving president not endorse the incoming candidate of their same party? Eventually, in March 2008, President George W. Bush endorsed John McCain.

Secondly, John McCain seemed "light-footed" when it came to debating Barrack Obama. Why is this? Here's my answer to that question, simply put: because of Obama's race. As a career politician, God forbid you attack a person of a minority race, because the repercussions would be your complete failure in DC politics, especially when you have to fight the mainstream media simultaneously. You have to understand; these days, if you are a Republican candidate, senator, congressman/woman, or a president, you're already labeled a racist, bigot, homophobe, xenophobe, in for the rich, and all in for Wall Street, etc., etc. This is the Democratic politician "playbook" and has been since the 1960s. John McCain knew this and resisted politically attacking Barrack Obama in any way, shape, or form. Even if the Republican candidate never says anything remotely prejudiced about his or her opponent, the mainstream media will spin it in order to make it so. So, since 2008, I have started paying more attention to DC politicians, and what they are willing to do or not do for the American people when it comes to their own careers.

In January 2009 Senator Barrack Obama became the forty-fourth president of the United States. "Hope and Change" was his campaign slogan. We never did receive the "hope" portion, but we definitely got the "change." When he said he was going to "fundamentally change our country," he wasn't bullshitting. Instead of delivering economic recovery, infrastructure, and immigration reform, as he campaigned on, he went way opposite. With a Democrat-controlled Senate, House of Representatives, and White House, we received a government-controlled healthcare system that turned out to be an utter failure. His administration could not get it started correctly, even through today's big technology. So, mine and millions of other

Americans' copays and premiums increased, millions of people were kicked off their previous insurance programs, and millions more lost their doctors of choice, just to name a few of the failures of the Affordable Care Act—more famously known as Obamacare. Let's not forget the mandate of the IRS punishing those who did not have health insurance by invoking a penalty between $1,000 to $1,200 for that tax year. I have a friend whose family owns a small bowling alley. At the time, they did not have health insurance and had to pay a large amount that they really couldn't afford.

Let us go forward to 2012: Benghazi, Libya, which went down on the anniversary of 9/11. Four Americans were killed, including a US ambassador, on a planned and well-executed terrorist attack led by Al Qaeda affiliates. This attack occurred towards the end of the 2012 presidential campaign between Barrack Obama and Massachusetts governor (at the time) Mitt Romney—another career politician. I'll go ahead and remind you of President Obama's reelection motto; it was "Osama Bin Laden is dead, General Motors is alive again, and Al Qaeda is on the run." Does that ring a bell for you?

Now, if an Al Qaeda–led attack occurred during his campaign, after he'd been promising the American voter that they were "on the run," it wouldn't look too good for his reelection. So he had Susan Rice, the United States ambassador for the United Nations at the time, go on several Sunday-morning and afternoon mainstream media channels to say that these attacks were provoked by an anti-Muslim YouTube video. Shortly after, reports steadily came in from the Department of Defense and the State Department that this was a random protest that "escalated out of control." Yeah, right—a protest with rocket-propelled grenades, machine guns, organized assault, and support elements being put in place? Fuck no it wasn't.

Anyone who has been in the military would tell you that this attack was clearly planned, organized, and rehearsed, despite the politicians' lies to the American people. Yes, they lied to the American people in order to save President Obama's narrative that foreign terrorism was "on the run," in order for him to win reelection. What's more, the secretary of state at the time, Hillary Clinton, received the intel and was asked for immediate support, but the leaders on the ground were denied for several hours.

Sometimes I say to my wife, "I don't know what pisses me off more—that they lie to us, or that they think we're stupid enough to believe them."

In 2012, with the Obamacare and Benghazi debacles slanting the election in his favor, Romney had this shit in the bag—seriously. But nope, he caved too, and screwed up his entire campaign. What really pissed a lot of us off was the fact that he kicked Obama's ass during the first debate. After that, not only did he hold back from pursuing the Benghazi attack on the debate stage, but he also didn't come back when Obama, very sarcastically and arrogantly, told him, "The 1980s wants their foreign policy back" when Romney stated that Russia was one of our biggest adversaries. Again, the Republican candidate caved, lost the election, and lost the American GOP voters' faith. Just another "slick" career politician who didn't have the balls to unleash on an opponent of a minority race.

Again, these are the views of almost seventy five million other "deplorables" across the flyover states. Now that you have a better understanding of where I stand, and how I got there, the following chapters will explain how I came to the conclusion in the title of this book.

CHAPTER 2

COMING DOWN THE ESCALATOR: HOPE FOR REAL HOPE & CHANGE

W hen I was a young boy, I would get off the school bus after an hour-long ride—because we lived out in the country in Lapeer, about ten miles outside of town—and walk into my house where my mother would be watching *The Oprah Winfrey Show*. We watched it together every day. Oprah used to have some interesting characters on her show, nothing like Phil Donahue, Geraldo Rivera, or even the outlandish daily scenes on the *Maury Povich Show*. Oprah had more conservative crowds and guests on her show, with none of the "soap-opera drama." In other words, no chair throwing or punching and fighting on her stage. No "you are or are not the father" moments. My mom and I loved Oprah Winfrey, especially after her debut performance in *The Color Purple*, which my mom took me to see at the Showcase Cinema in nearby Burton, just outside of Flint. She often took me to a matinee movie in the early afternoons when my dad was at work.

Every now and then, Oprah would have this young, good-looking, and occasionally arrogant guy on her show, dressed in a suit and tie.

I asked my mom who he was. She responded that he was some rich guy from New York. I asked her why Oprah kept having this guy on her show. My mom's reply was that they were good friends and he was a big businessman worth billions of dollars. It was Donald Trump, and he talked about how he felt the Soviet Union was not as much of a threat because President Reagan had them under control. He also told Oprah that China was a rising military and economic threat to the United States.

When she asked Donald if he had any desire to ever run for president, he responded with "Only if our country ever got that bad." Why would he ever run for president? He was a billionaire, living a billionaire's life. I think the president of the United States's salary is around $400,000 a year.

Once upon a time when they were friends.

In 2016, was our country bad off enough to need a New York businessman, and a nonpolitician, to run for president of the United States? Sixty-three million Americans said it was. In 2020, over seventy-four million still agreed.

Let's face it, the job market was very bad when I retired from the Army in 2010. Finding work in this country was not easy. I was turned away from three different management positions at Fortune 500 companies, and my resume from the military was shit hot, with seventeen years of leadership and managerial-duty positions. My wife was also turned down for several job opportunities, and she already had a master's in business , for Christ's sake. My point is that people in this country seem to forget how terrible the job market was during the Obama administration. Manufacturing jobs went overseas, big technical jobs were increasing, such as at Google, Facebook, Twitter, Apple, etc., and people with graduate-level degrees were humbling themselves by taking high-school-education-level jobs just to be able to work forty hours a week. These are only a few examples of what life was like during the first and into the second term of the Obama years.

That's not even counting the foreign affairs failures. Benghazi was only one aspect. With the complete US withdrawal from Iraq in 2011 came the rise of the Islamic State of Iraq and Syria (ISIS). Like I stated earlier, this 100 percent withdrawal went against every senior military leadership advisor's suggestion to President Obama—he did it anyway. Welcome to the entrance of ISIS into the Global War on Terrorism. As you all know, they marched across the heart of the Middle East, causing death, rape, and destruction as they invaded, pillaged, and captured land and its people. President Obama referred to them as the "junior varsity squad." He thought he was going to have a free pass on Middle East policies and the Global War on Terrorism because he gave the green light on the Osama Bin Laden raid on May 2, 2011. The reality was that his Middle East and other foreign policies led to the downfall of our national security and the security of sovereign nations across the globe. The "junior varsity squad" (ISIS) was left pretty much untouched under the Obama administration.

With the failed progress of the Affordable Care Act, the rise of ISIS in the Middle East, the divisions growing in our country, starting with the Ferguson, Missouri, police shooting, and how the Obama administration immediately politicized it and vilified law enforcement across the nation for it, we the people were growing tired. How about the scandals of the Internal Revenue Service going after conservative companies, or the dreadful Operation Fast and Furious led by the Department of Justice from 2009 to 2011, where two thousand US weapons were sold to Mexican buyers at the southern border in order to capture and arrest cartel criminals? The weapons couldn't be properly traced, and resulted in the murder of one of our own border patrolmen. He was murdered with a US-purchased weapon as part of the "covert-secret" operation under Eric Holder's Department of Justice. No culpability was acknowledged, not even an apology from the administration to the family of the victim.

Don't even get me started on Iran capturing our naval personnel in the Persian Gulf with no repercussions. Instead, the administration made the Iran deal, called the Joint Comprehensive Plan of Action, or the JCPOA, which also included us paying their regime 1.5 billion dollars in cash, in the middle of the night on an airstrip. We had the slowest-growing economy since the Great Depression, with more people on unemployment and food stamps, and the American people grew more pissed off weekly. Nobody was held accountable during those eight years. "Hope and Change" my ass. Again, I'm talking to you as a Middle-American, Northwest-Ohio-farmland "deplorable."

Here comes 2016 presidential candidate, New York businessman, billionaire, and host of the successful reality television program *The Apprentice* Donald J. Trump. When he and his wife first came down the escalator during the summer of 2015 and he announced he was running for president of the United States, it seemed to be a joke to a lot of the country, especially to the left-wing Democrats and the mainstream media. He was made fun of by many journalists and talk-show hosts, as if Trump were simply playing a game with the American people in a complete publicity stunt. A little over a year later, he became the forty-fifth president of the United States.

Let's talk about how he got there.

His initial announcement when he and his beautiful wife Melania Trump first stepped off the escalator at Trump Tower in New York unleashed the unending media criticism that this man would have to endure for the next five years. He and his entire family have been continuously scrutinized by 90 percent of the media in this country to this day, and probably will be for the remainder of their lives.

Hell, to be honest with you, I thought it was a joke at first. "Is the dude from *The Apprentice*, that I used to see on *Oprah* when I was a kid, really running for president?" However, in my opinion, a few things were certain with this man: our entire country knew who he was, that he always demanded excellent results, and that he would never be manipulated, bribed, or allowed to be coerced by anybody, or any organization, no matter how powerful they were believed to be. How can you bribe a billionaire from Queens, New York? It ain't happening, my friends.

I told my wife that this was going to be interesting; at the time, most Americans figured Jeb Bush was going to take this one because of his family's political dynasty. As a matter of fact, I told my wife that it was going to come down to Hillary and Jeb. Wow, was I wrong! Myself and many millions of others throughout our country.

It wasn't until the first primary debate that I told her that Donald Trump would not only be the primary GOP candidate but beat Hillary Clinton as well. We'll get into that in the next chapter.

During that initial announcement in 2015, Trump said a couple of main points that stuck with the right and completely got the left in an uproar. Number one was his comments on immigration and securing our southern border. You would have thought the man lined up a firing squad and began executing individuals, the way the media and the left carried on. They focused on his saying that many of the illegal aliens coming across our southern border were not good people—that many of them were drug dealers, human traffickers, rapists, and murderers. That they did not have merit to enter our country legally, so they were sneaking into our country illegally. I guess my question is, where was he wrong or statistically incorrect? The media immediately began restating and spinning his comment as "All Hispanics coming into our country from the southern border are rapists and murderers."

When he mentioned building a wall across the southern border to prevent illegal crossings from Mexico, he was immediately labeled a racist by the left and the media. I mean *immediately*. It was the old Democratic playbook, my friends. The left really lost their minds when he said that Mexico was going to pay for it. Did that mean Mexico was going to write the United States government a check? No, not at all. That's not even legal. Trump explained numerous times that there were other means of having Mexico pay for the wall, such as tariffs and trade negotiations, and also border-entry costs. Remember, this man was a lifetime trade and negotiation expert who dealt with foreign nations most of his adult life. The Democrats and the media always tried to convince us that we didn't know better, that we didn't know who this man was by now. They targeted him from the very beginning as an evil, racist person.

As a matter of fact, Donald Trump was friends with Al Sharpton for years, along with Jesse Jackson, the great Mohammad Ali, and many other African American leaders, including the niece of Dr. Martin Luther King Jr., Alveda King. Donald Trump was never accused by the left and the media of being a racist, homophobe, xenophobe, or a 'Nazi until he became the Republican primary candidate in summer 2016. Here's a quote from President Trump on Twitter after Al Sharpton wasted no time playing the "racist game" on him.

I have known Al for 25 years. Went to fights with him & Don King, always got along well. He "loved Trump!" He would ask me for favors often. Al is a con man, a troublemaker, always looking for a score. Just doing his thing. Must have intimidated Comcast/NBC. Hates Whites & Cops!

—President Donald Trump

Once upon a time when
they were friends.

Many people believe the 2011 White House Correspondents' Association dinner drove Donald Trump to run for president. At the invitation of the *Washington Post*, Trump attended the event, which essentially became a Donald Trump roast, minus the bad language. Trump's past comments and suggestions about someday possibly running for president became the theme.

President Obama started on him first, since Trump was one of the biggest advocates of the "birther movement"—basically, people who wanted to know if this sitting president was even an American citizen. It's funny when you think about it. Millions of Americans wanted to see Obama's birth certificate, just like those on the left want to see Trump's tax returns. I always asked my wife, "What are they going to find out, that Donald Trump is a rich billionaire?" I mean, the dude has only been on the scene for the last thirty or forty fucking years, right? It's not like he was some new person the entire world wasn't already familiar with.

Obama roasted Trump for almost five straight minutes. He said, "No one is happier, no one is prouder to put this birth certificate matter to rest than the Donald. That's because he can finally get back to focusing on the issues that matter, like: Did we fake the moon landing? What really happened in Roswell? And where are Biggie and Tupac?" These comments are mentioned in an article by Cleve R. Wootson Jr. that suggested this was the "breaking moment" when Trump decided to run for president of the United States.

I personally doubt it; I believe the breaking moment was the utter failure of the Mitt Romney campaign in 2012, as I mentioned previously. After that election, the conservative/GOP base in the United States realized there needed to be a change, and a major change in direction for the Republican Party if there was ever going to be another GOP president in our nation's future. A Washington outsider, perhaps, would be a last chance during the era of Obama and Hillary Clinton. Let's face it, the country already knew that Hillary was going to be the Democratic frontrunner. For a minute there, Bernie Sanders looked like he was going to make it, but we all know how that shit turned out. That dude didn't have a chance from the get-go.

More than two decades prior, another outsider who was not from the "DC machine" ran for president—Ross Perot. Remember that guy? He too was a billionaire businessman who challenged the status quo of DC politics. He ran as an independent during the 1992 Clinton and Bush (forty-one) campaign. Recently I watched several recaps on FOX News of him during the debates. It was actually sort of creepy to watch, and I don't mean creepy as in scary—more like uncanny. He was predicting events that have happened to our nation over the past few years. He called these facts almost thirty years ago. Somewhat of a Nostradamus scenario.

During the 1992 debates, he decried the North American Free Trade Agreement (NAFTA) that Bill Clinton was pitching to the American people. Perot argued that if a business could pay a person a dollar fifty an hour elsewhere versus thirteen or fourteen dollars an hour in the US, and have almost zero environmental and safety regulations, millions of manufacturing jobs in the United States would be leaving for Mexico and other countries like China. He was spot on.

Speaking of China, he warned that they had ambitions of becoming *the* global superpower. Nobody took Ross seriously back then because China was and is still considered to be a "developing nation." How, I have no idea. For as long as I can remember, many items I've owned, including clothing, have had a *Made in China* tag or sticker on them, and we can all relate to that. It's funny that the main people with the courage to warn our country about China in the past thirty years were two businessmen billionaires who were not career politicians. It makes you wonder, huh?

One thing was for sure by the summer of 2015: our nation was starving for a major change in our federal government, and especially in our White House.

CHAPTER 3

TRUMP VERSUS SIXTEEN OF THE TOP-GROOMED GOP ESTABLISHMENT CAREER POLITICIANS

onald Trump set the tone for the next four years, and he also changed the Republican Party for many years to come, if not forever. He did this during the first debate of the primary election. As a matter of fact, he did this right after the very first question of the debate, given to him by Fox News's Megan Kelly (when she was on that network, which she no longer is, but I'll talk about why in a little bit).

She asked him to explain why he had referred to women as pigs in the past. He interrupted her immediately and responded with, "Only Rosie O'Donnell." The crowd lost it and began cheering him on as if they were at a comedy roast; and that's exactly what it turned into. The debate turned into the "Donald Trump Roast," except the other sixteen candidates were the ones getting roasted by Trump. Megan tried to push back after his comedic, crowd-pleasing answer. So he gave her an ass chewing. He told her to her face that he didn't appreciate a question like that for a presidential candidate of the United States—that he knew she was trying to set him up for embarrassment and failure from the get-go. He turned it on her, embarrassing her in front of the crowd and millions of viewers across America. She NEVER got over it, even after he became the forty-fifth president. The debate immediately made clear that there were no apologies from this man; he was not going to be politically correct. Furthermore, he showed the country that he was not a politician—period.

After that initial exchange with Megan Kelly on live television, the next attack came from Senator Rand Paul, who called him out for not raising his hand when the question was asked if all candidates on the stage would concede to whoever won the primary vote. Donald Trump refused to raise his hand because his answer was simple. He said he would have to wait and see if the election was going to be fair to him, especially the Republican National Committee (RNC). If not, he would not be conceding. You have to understand that this man has been under scrutiny by politicians, particularly mayors and attorneys general from certain districts and cities, for most of his adult life as a businessman. He simply did not trust politicians.

When Rand Paul attempted to embarrass him, as Megan Kelly had, Trump shut him down quick. He interrupted his rant and said, "Hey, Rand, I've given your campaigns plenty of money in the past, so nice try." Rand shut his mouth immediately and turned red in the face as he looked down at his podium. He tried to go after Trump one more time, and again was knocked back down when Donald told him, "Hey, Rand, you might want to keep quiet over there. You're not having a very good night." Everyone on that stage who tried to shut him down in turn got embarrassed and annihilated by Mr. Trump. I thought I was watching *Celebrity Apprentice*! This was better than any soap opera or *Jerry Springer* episode I had ever seen.

The next contender was Jeb Bush. Jeb's big attack on him centered on the fact that Trump attended Chelsea Clinton's wedding years prior.

Jeb was trying to paint a picture that Trump was a traitor and not a *real serious Republican* because he had been friends with the Clintons for years at one point. Trump came back at him right away and said that not only did he attend the wedding, but also he had given donations to the Clintons in the past. He then embarrassed Jeb by stating that he had given money to both sides of the aisle, including giving to George W.'s campaigns twice. Trump scolded him, telling him that Trump was not a politician—that, as a businessman, you helped campaigns that you believed in for the better of the country. He then asked Jeb, "How did that turn out with that Iraq War thing, by the way?"

As soon as Donald mentioned his brother and the Iraq War, Jeb was done for the night.

Once upon a time when they were good friends.

Those were some of the highlights of the first primary election debate at the Quicken Loans Arena in Cleveland, Ohio, held on August 6, 2015. It was viewed on Fox News by twenty-four million viewers, making the debate the most-watched live broadcast for a non-sporting event in cable television history. When it was over, I told my wife that Trump would be the next president. She wasn't sure about that because he had to go up against Hillary eventually. I said that Hillary had too much baggage with the Benghazi attack and the ongoing email scandal. I and many others turned out to be right, but let's keep on the GOP primaries for now.

That first debate, the other sixteen candidates didn't know what to expect and thought they were going to play the typical politically correct game on a non-politically correct individual. One thing that Donald Trump proved that night was that he does not attack unless attacked first. When he does come back at you, he comes quickly and with a vengeance. He doesn't care what race, gender, or political status you have; you are not going to attack him without a good, solid fight. He has been consistent with this reputation his entire political career, all the way up to leaving office January 20, 2021.

The next day, he interviewed with a journalist, and to be honest with you, I cannot remember what network it was on, but he was asked why he was so hard on Megan Kelly. His response was simply put. He turned it around and asked why the first question asked of a presidential candidate would be a question like that—not a policy question, or a question on agenda for the nation to move forward, but a smear on his character from the start. I don't remember the exact quote, but I remember that the host tried to get an apology from him, and he wouldn't do it or fall for it. He was very sincere about what he believed to be the beginning of a campaign of character assassination against him because he was not and would never be politically correct. From that first question, I knew he would have an uphill battle. What I didn't realize was that he would have to endure this from the media, especially cable news, for the duration of his time in the District of Columbia as well.

Donald Trump was running against some popular politicians from the Republican establishment. Just a reminder for you, in case you forgot 2015 and the first half of 2016: There was governor of Ohio John Kasich, who to this day is a "Trump hater." Other than Mitt Romney, and of course every Democrat in the country, he is probably Trump's worst political enemy.

Then there was Senator Ted Cruz from Texas, who started an alliance with Trump in the beginning of the primaries, which as we all remember turned quickly when the race neared the end. Eventually, it all came down to the two of them, and it got very brutal at times with the verbal assaults. Trump even made a comment about Cruz's wife, if my memory serves me. The nicknames Donald came up with for many of his opponents amused his supporters. Senator Cruz's nickname was "Lying Ted." After he lost the primary, he decided to move forward with the Republican party and once again become allies with Trump. To this day Senator Cruz has been one of Trump's top supporters in Washington, DC.

Next came the senator from Florida, "Little Marco," which was Trump's nickname for Senator Marco Rubio. They too battled it out. Their most memorable back-and-forth was when Marco criticized Trump's small hands, and then made a reference that meant perhaps another portion of his body was small. Trump assured him "there was no problem in that area—trust me." Something to that effect. The crowd cheered and laughed. Every one of those debates always ended up as a comedy show, and the nation couldn't get enough of them. Later on, and to this day, Senator Rubio has supported President Trump 100 percent, and is another one of his loyalists on the DC scene.

Then came "Low-Energy Jeb," or former governor of Florida and little brother of former president George W. Bush, also son of former president George H. W. Bush, Jeb Bush. Trump "slapped him around" on those debate stages so much that it completely took him off the political stage, leading to the breakup of the Bush dynasty in US politics. To this day, Trump is public enemy number one to the Bush family. As president of the United States, Trump didn't even attend President George H. W. Bush's funeral services—in my opinion, not because he didn't respect him as a former president, but because it was obvious that he would not be welcome.

Carly Fiorina was the former CEO of Hewlett-Packard; therefore, theoretically, you can't put her in the "politician category." She too was a billionaire in the business world. The difference between her and Trump, however, was that Trump was self-made, and she was appointed by shareholders who called all the shots on how her company was being run. So, from a certain point of view, she was also a politician. Although Trump never gave her one of his famous nicknames, he did tweet something about her face in a derogatory manner, and the media went ape-shit over it. That was supposed to be the "final straw" that would forever end him and his campaign, because now he was a complete "sexist." Nope, it didn't end him.

I won't bore you by giving descriptions of every other Republican candidate running against Donald Trump during the 2016 GOP primary election. There was also governor of New Jersey Chris Christie, who came off the campaign and immediately endorsed Donald Trump. The same with former governor of Virginia Jim Gilmore, Senator Rick Santorum from Pennsylvania, former governor of Arkansas Mike Huckabee, former governor of Wisconsin Scott Walker, former governor of Louisiana Bobby Jindal, and last but not least, Senator Lindsey Graham. Lindsey has disagreed with President Trump on certain issues but in my opinion has been one of the top loyalists during Trump's entire time as a candidate and as president. He, like Ted Cruz and Marco Rubio, is loyal to this day.

Two former GOP candidates were eventually selected by Trump to be part of his cabinet at the White House when he won in November 2016: former governor of Texas Rick Perry, and Dr. Ben Carson. Dr. Carson served the entire four years of the Trump presidency as secretary of housing and urban development (HUD). Rick Perry was selected by Trump to be his secretary of energy. All former candidates mentioned in the previous paragraphs remained loyal to President Trump during his presidency, except for Bush, Fiorina, and definitely Kasich. As a matter of fact, and again I'm getting a little ahead of myself, John Kasich announced that he would vote for Joe Biden in the 2020 election, and he did. Now that's hatred for Trump if I've ever seen it.

After that first debate, Donald Trump was a guest on *The View*. Yes, believe it or not, he was loved by the left at one time. If you weren't raised in the '80s or '90s, you would never know it, but many people still remembered when Donald Trump supported the Democrat Party. The ladies on the show loved him and treated him with the utmost respect. Yeah, they asked him some challenging questions, but nothing like you've seen in the past four or five years. The ladies were intrigued by how he didn't take any of the other candidates' shit on the debate stage. Many on the left were impressed by how he attacked some of the biggest names of the Republican Party, live on television.

The show quickly became a gateway for the ladies, in particular Joy Behar and Whoopi Goldberg, to attempt to convince Donald to run as an independent candidate. Remember when I said that Ross Perot ran as an independent during the Bush Sr. and Bill Clinton campaigns? Ross's run that year pretty much cost Bush the election. I believe the ladies on *The View* were trying to convince Trump to do the same, hoping it would have the same outcome as 1992. Trump did not fall for it. He was cordial with the ladies, and replied with his famous "We'll see what happens," but they wouldn't let it go.

This was when I realized that the left was getting concerned with this man running, fearing he was a potential threat to Hillary Clinton's campaign. Like I said, that first debate made everyone raise an eyebrow—this man scared the shit out of them. That was the last time Donald Trump was ever invited on that program, but his name was mentioned every day on it for the next five years, with pure hatred. I would estimate that *The View* was the most Trump-hating program on a regular television network other than cable news; it still is.

Once upon a time when they were good friends.

Let's talk about the battle between Donald Trump and Senator John McCain. This battle goes back a couple of decades. In January 2000, Trump was on CBS, talking about someday running for president, just as he had on *The Oprah Winfrey Show* fifteen years prior. Trump was asked about Senator John McCain making a run for president as well. Of course, whenever someone brought up the late senator from

Arizona, they always mentioned his war service, and what he had to endure in Vietnam as a prisoner of war.

Trump criticized McCain's war service. "He was captured," Trump said, in remarks he would echo years later during his primary campaign run. "Does being captured make you a hero? I don't know. I'm not sure." When Trump announced he was running for president in 2015, McCain immediately distanced himself from the real estate tycoon. He said that he strongly disagreed with Trump's comments that Mexicans were "rapists," again misrepresenting what came out of Trump's mouth that day he came down the escalator. Senator McCain was playing the role of a career politician.

In July 2015, during a rally in McCain's home state of Arizona, Trump claimed that Senator McCain was weak on immigration. He also called out the senator for not doing enough for the veterans of our nation, especially after the deaths of veterans who were put on long waiting lists to be seen at the VA hospitals in Arizona. Of course, this fueled the fire, and McCain came back at him. Later that same month, most Americans caught their first glimpse of the feud when Trump, speaking in Iowa, questioned whether McCain was a war hero because he was captured. Trump said, "I liked people that weren't captured." That not only fired up McCain, of course, but fired up a lot of us who have served.

I was not happy with Trump for making those comments. I actually thought that was going to be the end of his campaign. Most men would never be able to make it through the torture John McCain did. For Donald Trump, who had not served in Vietnam, to make that bold comment was a blunder that I believe stuck with him throughout his entire presidency. It certainly did with the entire McCain family, and rightfully so—in particular, his daughter Meghan McCain, who also was a co-host with Fox News at the time.

Our country was so starved for real change for the better that Donald Trump was forgiven for his comments. I would be the first to tell you, as would many other Trump supporters across our nation, that I'm not a fan of some of the stuff that comes from that man's mouth. There were many moments when I turned to my wife and said, "Fuck! I wish he would just keep his mouth shut!"

Okay, now that I have that off my chest, let's move on. After all the battles and debates with Marco Rubio and Ted Cruz, Donald Trump became the Republican presidential candidate in June 2016. We (his supporters) had hope for his chances of becoming the forty-fifth president of the United States, and we were pumped—I don't need to remind you, if you can remember the size of the crowds he was drawing at his rallies. He's had the same-size crowds during the last five years, whether he was rallying for himself or another Republican seat in either the Senate or the House, including state governor seats.

Here comes Hillary Clinton—former First Lady, former senator from New York, and former secretary of state. Trump immediately nicknamed her "Crooked Hillary." Like I told you earlier, Donald Trump does not care about race, gender, or anyone's political status; he is going to attack you if you attack him. The only difference is he's going to do it ten times harder. Donald Trump had defeated the "Bush dynasty." Now he had to take on the "Clinton machine" for the seat in the Oval Office. This was not going to be an easy task because the Clintons *were* Washington, DC. They had been part of and "the leaders" of the Washington establishment for many, many years. They were beloved within "the swamp." They were "the queen and king" of the Democratic Party and had all the support and money to back it too. As a matter of fact, they were so powerful that the Democratic National Committee (DNC) purposely maneuvered Senator Bernie Sanders out of the Democrat primaries in the spring of 2016. As a reminder, Bernie is a self-proclaimed Democratic Socialist. I guess he was getting too much support from the younger and upcoming voters. I mean, you can only offer so much free stuff before socialism starts sounding pretty good to kids. The DNC were caught with leaked emails from Congresswoman and then chairman of the committee Debbie Wasserman Schultz, who was forced to resign after it was discovered that she was working against Bernie Sanders on behalf of Hillary Clinton. The establishment was even too big for "the Bern."

Just like the Benghazi scandal, the recent email scandal, and the Clinton Foundation "pay to play" scandal, nobody seemed to care. Nobody cared because it was Hillary Clinton, and she was being groomed to be the forty-fifth president and first female president of the United States. After all, it was her turn, and she was "owed the presidency," right? She was supposed to win it in 2008, but that damn Barrack Obama got in her way. She just could not talk to people and convince them that she had the charisma or drive to be the president.

Going back to the email scandal, she was caught sending hundreds of classified emails over her private server while she was secretary of state under Barrack Obama. Now, to the average person reading this, it's like so what, who cares, right? Let me break down the severity of that crime in my terms so that one can truly understand what could happen to the average person if they got caught, as she did, doing this.

As a high-ranking person in the military with a top secret government clearance, if I had sent one email with classified information through my Yahoo account, I would have received a minimum sentence of at least ten years in federal prison. That's right, I would have gotten a nice long vacation at the illustrious Fort Leavenworth, Kansas, where I would be staring up at fifty-foot concrete walls and making big rocks into little rocks. So, you can see where the frustration of millions in this country comes from with the double standard that gives one side of the aisle free passes. I'm mean, for Christ's sakes, Ted Kennedy drove off a bridge while he was drunk driving, causing his friend and passenger to drown, and remained in the US Senate for almost fifty years—untouched.

James Comey, director of the FBI at the time of the investigation on her email scandal, pretty much gave her a free pass. The funny part was that the fucking FBI doesn't have the authority to dismiss a crime, hence why they are called Bureau of Investigation. It is up to the attorney general whether or not to charge someone who was a former cabinet member. Oh, by the way, at the time that was Loretta Lynch, who secretly met with former president Bill Clinton on an airport tarmac. When asked by the press why she found it necessary to meet with the former president in private, she claimed they were simply talking about their grandchildren. Yeah right.

After their meeting, James Comey mysteriously dismissed the investigation on Hillary, claiming there was not enough proof for criminal charges. She went on to be the Democrat primary candidate against Donald Trump.

Earlier that spring, our two children both completed their confirmation here in North Baltimore at our Catholic church. My parents came down from Michigan to attend the ceremony and spent the night at our house. After we left the church, my parents and friends came over to my house to celebrate with beverages, cake, and ice cream. We had a great party, and everyone had a fun time, especially the kids when it was time for them to open their cards and gifts.

After the party was over and everyone left, my parents, me, and my wife, Jessica, hung out in my kitchen. Lo and behold, and I don't remember who brought it up first, the current political situation got mentioned. My mother didn't really say a whole lot, but we weren't arguing. I could tell she was nervous, probably afraid that it would get hostile, which it never did. We kept the conversation going for almost two hours without animosity. We just went back and forth, disagreeing with one another about Donald Trump versus Hillary Clinton.

I pretty much told my dad everything I've told you up to this point. He didn't want to hear it or have any part of it, and I understand why. They have been Democrats their entire lives, and that was the end of it. No ifs, ands, or buts. What I was trying to get through to them that night was that the Democratic Party they grew up with no longer exists. The days of the JFK Democrats and even Bill Clinton are gone, and are not coming back. Hell, in today's political world, Bill Clinton would have been considered a Republican, especially considering how the far left has taken over the Democratic Party.

People have challenged me on Facebook to give them examples of why I believe this. I'll give you one now—his welfare reform policy. If you remember, during his first term in office, President Clinton made it mandatory that anyone receiving any government subsidy had to conduct some type of community service or work program, such as cleaning or volunteer work in homeless shelters, etc. I believe they had to volunteer twenty or thirty hours a week. That shit would NEVER happen today with a Democrat presidency. That's a fact! Clinton's policy pissed off the left so bad that Michael Moore based his first movie off of it. Now, I don't have to tell you that if Michael Moore is writing and directing a movie about how fucked up he thinks your policy is, you're probably a conservative or have conservative views.

During my conversation with my parents, I realized that facts and history don't matter; once someone is committed to a certain political party, that's it—there's no changing anyone's mind. I did back in 2004 because policies concerning my service to our nation affected me personally. I even mentioned that to my dad. I think during the eight years of President Clinton's time as my commander in chief, the military received maybe two small raises. With George W. Bush, we were getting a raise every year. Anyone who has ever served on active duty military knows that we don't make a lot of money. If you're enlisted like I was, you really don't see a comfortable monthly paycheck until you hit the rank of E-7.

Eventually, we ended our discussion as it started to get somewhat heated. When we all went to bed that night, I realized that this was going to happen more and more with my family. Not only with my parents, but eventually with my brother as well, especially since we had already debated on Facebook about Obama's policies throughout his presidency.

I'll be completely honest with you now, and I'll get into this a little more in the upcoming chapters of this book, but I have not spoken to or seen my parents or brother in four years now. Yes, I am part of that statistic you've heard and read about, where family members break up over this shit. Not just my immediate family, but cousins too—oh yeah.

Okay, getting back to the 2016 presidential general election between Donald Trump and Hillary Clinton. She first went after him by trying to convince voters that he was clueless on foreign affairs and foreign policies. Her status as a former senator and secretary of state, in her mind, was enough to convince the same voters that she had all the experience. What she didn't take into consideration was her poor record on foreign affairs. She walked herself right into that one. Trump annihilated her immediately on her failed foreign policies. The only word that he had to bring up was *Benghazi*. That quieted her down immediately. She definitely didn't want that shit brought back up, especially after it seemed to have cooled down in the past few years. It didn't cool down with Donald Trump or the sixty-three million voters he had either.

She then tried to convince Americans that he was going to be an anti-military president. She always brought up his twenty-year scuffle with Senator McCain. She reminded the voters about Trump's previous comments on the "hero" thing, and attempted to make McCain seem like a victim. I always say, "I love the way the left always thinks that everyone has amnesia for some reason"—like we all forgot what they said about McCain when he was the GOP candidate for president. He was called a racist, homophobe, all in for the rich and Wall Street, etc. You know, again, the "Democrat playbook." Now that he had publicly made his negative feelings for Trump known, all of a sudden he was a war hero and the next best thing since sliced bread to the same people who badmouthed him eight years prior.

Trump continuously called her out on all these subjects too. I mean twenty-four seven, around the clock. By this time, we had all figured out that the man did not sleep, and kept going and going, and then when he was done going, he would go some more. Hillary and the Clinton family as a whole were not used to anyone calling them out like this man was doing to her and her husband. I mean, let's face it, they were the elite of the elitists of the DC machine.

She would attack him for his demeanor, and he would come back at her for her character faults, including sticking up for her husband and denigrating the women who had accused him of sexual assault in the past. I still remember the debate (I think it was the last one) where he had three of the ladies who had accused Bill Clinton of sexual assault during his time as Arkansas governor sitting in the first row as his guests in order to intimidate Hillary while they were battling it out on stage. Like I said, go after him time and time again, and he will retaliate like a ruthless warrior.

I think the best line of any of the three debates came after Hillary asked the commentators and the crowd if they could imagine a Trump presidency in charge of a modern-day Department of Justice. Without hesitation, and quick on his feet as he has been his entire adult life, Trump replied with, "Because you'd be in jail." I don't know what offended her more—that line or the crowd when they began cheering. I'm telling you, no matter what you think of the debates, they were better than any reality show or soap opera.

Outside of the debates, Trump constantly tore Hillary down, and she did the same to him, especially every time she showed up on any talk show or interview. *The View* loved her, as did *60 Minutes, Good Morning America*, and pretty much every other news organization— although I don't look at *The View* as a news show; it's more a small handful of individuals gossiping with their left-wing agendas.

Donald always seemed to attack his opponents' drive, or lack thereof, such as Jeb Bush and now "Crooked Hillary." He said that she would wake up in the morning, conduct a television interview, go back to her hotel, and take a three-hour nap. I used to laugh and ask my wife, "Where the hell does he come up with this shit?" How about the time when she was dehydrated and almost collapsed on her way to her limousine? That was not a good look for her. Her Secret Service detail had to catch her and physically place her into the vehicle. I don't think the mainstream media even covered it, but Fox News Channel sure did. God knows, had that been Trump, that would have been on every news network for forty-eight hours straight. Let's face it, Trump was the media's, Hollywood's, higher academia's, the East and West Coast elitists', and obviously the entire Democratic Party's public enemy number one.

So, here is my summary of how the media formed their opinion of Donald Trump. Back when he was the New York businessman, Democrat, and the host of *Celebrity Apprentice*, he was practically beloved. When he announced he was running for president in 2015, he was considered a joke. When he started winning the GOP debates, he startled the left. When he officially won the candidacy in 2016, he was immediately vilified as a demon, and remains so to this day. This sequence reminds me of what Mel Gibson told Jim Caviezel while they were filming *The Passion of the Christ*; Gibson warned Caviezel that if he decided to take the role of Jesus Christ, he would never be offered a job in Hollywood again. When did Hollywood move so far to the left that they began looking down on Christianity, especially since one of the most famous Democratic presidents, JFK, was Catholic? Oh, by the way, Joe Biden is our second Catholic president. How's that going to work out?

Getting back to the 2016 general election, Hillary was just not connecting with the American people, particularly blue-collared Middle America. I don't think she had a message other than "I'm going to be the first female president, and Donald Trump is a bad person." That was not resonating with anyone, except, of course, for the hardcore forever Democrats of the nation. Honestly, I believe a lot of them stayed home that November because she wasn't resonating with them either.

Hillary had three big failures during her campaign: Number one was her mouth. The "deplorables" comment lost her half the nation. Number two, she said at a town hall that she would see to it that the coal industry was put out of business, ensuring that thousands of coal miners would lose their jobs. I said to my wife, "Well, she just lost southern Ohio, West Virginia, Pennsylvania, and Kentucky"—and she did. Who the hell campaigns by threatening to put people out of work, no matter what industry they are in? Apparently, she thought it was a smart move. A week later, she was at a restaurant in West Virginia, I believe, and attempted to backpedal her comment when she was confronted by a voter.

The second of her major failures was her arrogant composure when it came to answering questions from not only the media but also voters during town hall meetings, or when she was simply going to restaurants and in public in general. She came off as fake. Remember when she was down in one of the Southern states? I believe it was Louisiana or perhaps Alabama, and she was campaigning and doing a town hall within a predominately black community. She began answering questions in a Southern Black dialect. Then she went on a Black radio talk show not too long after and claimed that she always travels with a bottle of hot sauce in her purse. Seriously? Talk about stereotyping a race of people.

Episodes like this opened the American people's eyes to the fact that the Democrats only go into these minority communities every two and four years to get votes—part of the playbook: Campaign in these communities, put on a show that you are totally on their side and going to help them with every problem they face on a daily basis, and once you convince them of that, convince them that your Republican opponent is a racist. Every Democrat candidate has been doing it for decades. Once they receive the vote from the minority community, they'll leave like ghosts, never accomplishing anything for those neighborhoods or their inhabitants' livelihoods.

Don't take my word for it. The cities of Detroit, Flint, and Saginaw of my home state of Michigan used to be the industrial capitals of the world. Unfortunately, they have been run by these same empty promises from Democrat mayors for the past seventy years and then some. God forbid many of these far-left mayors or state governors get into DC. I've said this for the longest time: the fastest way to become a millionaire in this country isn't working towards owning a business or becoming a musician, actor, or any other type of artist. It's becoming a DC politician. Shit, they make an average of two to three hundred thousand a year. Show me a career congressman/woman or a senator who isn't worth millions these days. Why do you think they never want to leave DC?

Hillary's third major failure during the 2016 general election was neglecting to travel to certain states. She did this probably because they were historically blue states—states like Michigan, Wisconsin, and Pennsylvania, all of which she lost the night of the election. She took these states for granted and believed they would be automatic wins for her. Donald Trump, however, was holding major rallies in major cities in those exact states. At the end of the day, he worked his ass off, and out-campaigned her by a mile. The results of his efforts and energy during that summer, going into the fall, was apparent—he would be the victor of this presidential race.

On the night of November 8, 2016, I went to bed around 11 p.m. The polls had Hillary ahead of Donald, but those same polls showed that he was still moving forward. I figured it was going to be close but that she was going to win the normal blue states, which would have put Donald out of the competition. The media thought so too. I woke up around 5:30 the next morning to discover that Donald Trump won the election. I was extremely happy, as were sixty-three million other American voters. Watching the left-wing news, you would have thought we were witnessing an apocalypse. CNN and MSNBC lost it. Their journalists were even dropping f-bombs live on their networks. Megan Kelly and Brett Baier from Fox News were covering the election results that day and throughout the evening, and you could almost see the tears in Megan's eyes as Brett announced that Donald J. Trump was going to be the forty-fifth president of the United States.

Speaking of this former anchor at Fox News, Megan Kelly was on prime time at 7 p.m. During the entirety of the primary and general elections in 2016, she had guests and analysists on her show who would bash Donald Trump for pretty much her entire hour on air every night. It got to the point where I thought that I was watching MSNBC or CNN. There was a time when I thought that she was a "fair and balanced" former lawyer with a strong head for what was right and wrong. After that first primary debate, she never got over her hatred of this man. President Donald Trump even accepted an invitation to a one-on-one interview with her after the 2016 election. I'm not sure if she expected an apology from him or what, but she never received it, though he was cordial and treated her with respect.

Not too long after President Trump entered the White House, and I don't think it was even six months into his presidency, Megan Kelly was off Fox News. People on the left will argue that Fox News only wants conservative views on their programs. Not true. In the case of Megan Kelly, her show was nothing but a Trump-bashing hour, night after night, week after week, and month after month. If she felt that way, then she should have taken herself to MSNBC or CNN. I believe she ended up on a morning show on NBC.

After Trump became president-elect, people were shown on news channels with tears pouring out of their eyes. Nobody was more upset with the results than Hillary herself—obviously. She never did accept her loss. For the past four years she has continued to go before crowds and give every excuse for why she unfairly lost. I wonder sometimes what is going on in her head now that Joe Biden has won the 2020 election. She probably loses sleep every night, wondering how Biden was able to beat Trump and she could not. I'll give you my theory a little later.

On January 20, 2016, Donald J. Trump was sworn in as the forty-fifth president of the United States. There were simultaneous protests from the left throughout Washington, DC. Many Democrats from the House of Representatives and the Senate refused to attend his inauguration ceremony on the steps of the US Capitol. We were truly a divided county at this point.

CHAPTER 4

AN EXCELLENT FOUR-YEAR PRESIDENCY AND AN UPHILL BATTLE

The forty-fifth president of the United States,
Donald J. Trump.

W ithin the first hour and a half of his being in the Oval Office, some Democrat representatives and senators were already calling for the impeachment of President Trump. Trump supporters were outraged. "Impeach him for what?" The man literally just stepped into the White House.

My point is that the bullshit started immediately. At the time, Nancy Pelosi was the House minority leader, and Paul Ryan from Wisconsin was the Speaker of the House. The Republicans had the majority in both houses of Congress, and now the White House. The future was bright for our nation.

President Trump went straight to work with signing executive orders. His first priority was to rebuild our job market. To do that, two things had to happen: he had to cut environmental and labor regulations, and then had to lower the corporate tax rate, which would require a bill passed from the House and then the Senate. Once it reached his desk, he would sign it into law. It was like the damn *School House Rock* video: "I'm just a bill, yes, I'm only a bill, and I'm sitting here on Capitol Hill."

Trump cut hundreds of restrictive manufacturing regulations through executive order. This was the first step in the right direction to start bringing these jobs back from overseas. As this was going on, Paul Ryan developed a bill to cut not only corporate but individual income taxes as well. This bill also included termination of the mandate from the IRS to penalize individuals and/or families for not having health insurance. This new bill killed two birds with one stone, and the American people were relieved, especially those who did not have health insurance.

On top of regulation and tax cuts, President Trump also had meetings with CEOs across the nation to discuss bringing their factories back to Michigan, Ohio, and other parts of the country. Many of them did just that. He was accomplishing this while he was still president-elect. He talked an air-conditioning company into moving from Mexico back to Indiana, resulting in about a thousand new jobs for that community—before he was even in the White House.

He got the tax-cut bill passed into law, and the job market took off big-time. The corporate tax rate went down from 35 percent to 21. He wanted to take it down to 15 percent, but Pelosi and Chuck Schumer weren't having it. So, Trump settled. This caused job growth throughout the country, pay increases, and income taxes to lower. Bonuses were given out by many companies to their employees, including large annual bonuses.

Of course, Nancy Pelosi had to shit all over it, and why? Because it was under Trump's watch. Man, she hated that man right from the beginning. She referred to the paychecks and bonuses that people were getting as "crumbs." Give me a break. This woman was worth over three hundred million dollars, so I guess according to her rich self, it would be crumbs. My wife received her largest bonus that year from CSX Railroad, and trust me, it was up there. It certainly wasn't crumbs to us. Not to mention our income taxes went down, especially hers because she was paying almost 30 percent monthly. Mine barely went down because my monthly pay is military active duty retirement, so I was paying under 7 percent. Either way, combined as a household, that meant around $250 extra a month.

The reason I'm putting this out there is primarily because I want people to know how the Trump tax cuts directly affected my household. Friends on social media argued with me that $250 extra a month wasn't shit. Well, the way my wife and I looked at it, that additional monthly income paid for my daughter's car payment while she was attending college. What the hell is the problem with that? Every little bit helps. My mom actually complained and made fun of their income tax decrease on Facebook, comparing theirs to "the amount of a cup of coffee a day." Again, my dad earns a pension from the state of Michigan, so yes, if you pay less than 8 or 7 percent income tax a month, you're not going to see a big difference every month. Anything to bash this administration, right? If the tax cuts had come from Barrack Obama or Hillary Clinton, it would have been a "reward," no matter what the monthly pay increase was.

One thing nobody can argue against, however, is that the job market increased and unemployment decreased. A family member tried to convince me that it was only minimum-wage jobs. Not true, but so what if it were? The unemployment rate is the unemployment rate. Nothing for the left is ever good enough when a Republican is in charge of making something happen to help the country, especially the blue-collar middle class.

On January 24, 2017 (four days into office), President Trump signed the executive order to approve and begin construction of the Keystone/ XL Pipeline that runs from Canada through the United States and down to Texas. He approved the Dakota Pipeline as well. This not only created approximately eleven thousand union jobs for both the US and Canada but also sealed the deal to free the United States from oil dependency on OPEC and the Middle East. Within Trump's first year, the US became energy independent for the first time in seventy years. Simultaneously, he signed the order to open government-owned protected land in Alaska for oil drilling and fracking. This created more energy independence for the US, and again created more jobs.

After the job market took off and the economy began improving, President Trump's next priority and promise he made during his campaign was to rebuild our military. Our tanks were old, as were the planes and ships. We were still using tanks built in the late 1970s. Our small arms were old as well. With nearly three trillion dollars, his administration completely rebuilt the military, with all the equipment made in the United States. He then created and launched the first brand-new branch of our Armed Forces in over seventy-five years—the Space Force.

Of course, with the cost to rebuild our services came additional spending from the Democrats in Congress. There was so much crap and "pork spending" included in the proposed budget that it made the president's head spin. I remember he was pissed when he read the bill, but he signed it anyway, primarily because he had to get our military new equipment. He told the Democrats that he would never sign anything like that again. He only signed it for the sake our service members.

With a rebuilt military, it was time to deal with North Korea once and for all. Kim Jong-un continued to launch test rockets across parts of Asia, primarily Japan, and he was also threatening the citizens of Guam. Per his family history, of course he continued to threaten South Korea as well. During the transition of power to Donald Trump from the Obama administration, President Obama told him that the biggest problem he was going to face during his presidency was North Korea.

Now, one thing you must remember when it comes to dealing with North Korea is that we are still technically at war with them. In 1953, the United States, South Korea, North Korea, and even China signed the Armistice Agreement, or basically a cease fire, which is still in effect to this day. We've had approximately thirty thousand troops in South Korea ever since, including the Demilitarized Zone, or DMZ, along the border of the two Koreas, in preparation for war against North Korea if their government ever decides to attack the south again.

The Korean War never officially ended. Today, there is still no peaceful settlement between these two nations. South Korea is a flourishing, peaceful democratic society with a strong economy, while North Korea remains a hard-line communist country that is strongly sanctioned by the free world—led by the United States. One thing that these two nations' governments have in common is that for them the Korean War is ongoing.

In March 1997, I got assigned to the 1st Battalion, 506th Parachute Infantry Regiment (Air Assault), 2nd Infantry Division, in South Korea. I was levied from Fort Bragg, North Carolina, to do a year-long hardship tour in Korea. Getting levied is a nice way of saying "drafted." Back in those days, before the Army went totally digital, you would get a notification in the mail. The unit you were assigned to would also be notified that you had a permanent change of station (PCS) with a tentative report date.

At the time I received my PCS orders for Korea, I was a sergeant and a team leader assigned to the 82nd Airborne Division. I still remember when the first sergeant called me down to his office and told me the "bad news."

"Sergeant Augi, I just received a levy notice on you for Korea," he said with a sorry tone.

I replied, "What the fuck, First Sergeant? I just got assigned to your company six months ago."

"Yeah, but how long have you been here on Fort Bragg?"

"A little over three years now."

"Okay, that's why you got levied. The Army tends to move soldiers around every three years or so. Your time was up, young man. Don't worry about it. Most of us have to do our time in Korea. I've been there twice."

"When do I have to report?"

"No later than March 1. So, after we get back from our month in Panama in January, you can prepare to clear the unit, the post, and go on PCS leave."

"Roger that, First Sergeant," I replied.

I walked down the hallway, shaking my head in disbelief. I had already served an overseas tour in Germany prior to Bragg, and I did not wish to do another one. Sometimes the military doesn't deal you the cards you want, but that's life. In February 1997, I signed out of Fort Bragg and went on a thirty-day PCS leave back home to Michigan in preparation for a year in Korea.

I got stationed along the DMZ. I remember we could see the North Korean flag from our battalion headquarters on Camp Greaves. Huge speakers from the North would echo propaganda twenty-four hours a day towards the South, which was kind of creepy, not to mention obnoxious. The Imjin River was the northernmost point in South Korea that the civilian population could go. Freedom Bridge was the final structure leading across the river to the DMZ. I pulled guard on it twice during my year on the peninsula. It was a week-long duty. It was me, a Katusa (Korean Augmentation to the United States Army), a South Korean Army sergeant, a South Korean Army soldier, and a South Korean intelligence agent. Katusas were South Korean soldiers placed in the ranks of the US Army. In an infantry platoon, there would normally be at least one Katusa per squad. The word was that they usually came from families with enough money to put them in the US Army instead of the brutal South Korean Army, where regular abuse took place. In South Korean law, every capable male must serve a minimum of two years within their military. Remember, they were still at war with North Korea.

The warlike mentality was very evident when I got over there; all main bridges for rivers and roads were mined. Checkpoints were on every highway and main road throughout the entire country, and there were definitely more when you got closer to the DMZ. The Imjin River itself was heavily mined. You never saw any boats traveling through it, at least in the area of Freedom Bridge.

Me on Freedom Bridge guard duty on the Imjin River; 1997, DMZ Korea

Within the first two hours of any soldier getting to their unit (at least in our battalion), the standard was to get a protective mask (gas mask) and weapon assigned. The leadership, usually a squad leader or team leader, would take the newly assigned soldier around our camp and show him his assigned bunker in the event we were attacked with indirect fire from the North. All this was done before the soldier even got assigned a room in the barracks. Then, after he was in-processed fully, his team leader would take him to his room, get his rucksack put together to our standard, and pack it fully with our packing list. After that was done, the team leader would take him up for his initial ass smoking on "Magic Mountain." This was a five or six-mile hike straight uphill in the dark. We were in Alpha Company, 1st Battalion, 506th Parachute Infantry Regiment, and it was the most physically exhausting unit I was ever assigned to in my twenty years in the Army.

So, President Trump's dealing with the communist dictator Kim Jong-un from North Korea was personal to me and other veterans who have served on that peninsula since 1950. I watched news on the events taking place in that region of the world every day, anticipating possible war and our new president's response to Chairman Kim's threats. This was where our country and the world would discover whether Donald Trump was a warmonger or a peacemaker. I still like to refer to his mentality as being that of peace through strength: Do not fuck with us because you'll pay severely. However, we would rather work with you to help your nation achieve a better way of life.

This was a test of the United States' new president, and the whole world knew it. Everyone also knew that the United States could annihilate North Korea. I believe one of Trump's famous tweets on Twitter that got the left in an uproar went something like, "If one of their nuclear weapons are launched, Pyongyang would be underwater in a matter of an hour." At this point, Trump had ordered an additional aircraft carrier and several nuclear submarines off the coast of the peninsula. The exact number was classified, of course, but I'm sure it was significant since our president seemed pretty confident.

Kim knew this to be true and pulled back the reins on his military conducting any more testing of rockets, cooling down his threats to South Korea, Japan, and Guam. The United States has troops with their families stationed in all three of these countries. Any attack on these countries would be a declaration of war against us. Kim definitely did not want that. No country would.

Once everything calmed down between our two nations, Trump reached out to Kim Jong-un for a meeting on peace negotiations. The left completely lost their minds over this, as they did about everything else Donald Trump attempted and accomplished for his entire presidency. First they called him a warmonger for escalating forces in the region. Then they went after him for trying to negotiate peace with Kim. Let's not forget, during this time the Russian-collusion investigation was hot and heavy, and now Pelosi, Schumer, and the mainstream media were telling the American people that President Trump was coddling dictators. Anything to shit all over everything he was trying to accomplish, right?

Once Chairman Kim got the hint that President Trump wasn't fucking around with him, he began making promises to the United States. For example, he stopped all missile testing (for that initial period), he promised to meet with the South Korean president, and he also promised to find and return US soldiers' remains from the Korean War to the United States. Trump held back to see if he was going to be true to his word, and he was. The chairman also returned US citizens in captivity in labor camps across North Korea (I believe it was three citizens at the time). I couldn't imagine what they had to endure in that environment.

Once all that happened, Trump agreed to meet him in person to begin negotiating dismantling of their nuclear weapons. Again, the left criticized his efforts. Chuck Schumer stood on the Senate floor and basically said that President Trump was wasting his time and would be caving to Chairman Kim, which never happened. One thing again that I could never understand with Pelosi or Schumer: How did they always think that this man was going to be weak on negotiation? I think what really pissed me and half the country off was the fact that according to every Democrat in Washington, DC, he was prone to fail in his negotiations and communication with other countries' leadership. The fact of the matter is they strongly wished that he would fail at all costs rather than achieve a major win.

It was a chance for hope that North Korea would get rid of their nuclear weapons and eventually make peace with South Korea, officially ending the war almost seventy years after the cease-fire. Furthermore, millions of families on both sides of the DMZ had been separated from loved ones for decades and wished to reunite. The negotiation provided the hope the world wanted, except probably China. China has always had a strong grip on North Korea.

On June 12, 2018, President Trump and Chairman Kim Jong-un attended the North Korean–United States Singapore Summit, commonly known as the Singapore Summit. President Trump was the first US president to ever meet face-to-face with a North Korean chairman in history. This chance for a new beginning was seen live across the globe. The two met, shook hands, and seemed to be pleasant with one another.

President Trump presented Chairman Kim with a slideshow on his intentions for future relations between the United States and North Korea. Trump assured him that he was seeking not regime change of the hard-line communist nation but rather to someday open up positive relations and trade as we had with South Korea. The US demanded only one thing with this optimistic deal—North Korea MUST get rid of all their nuclear weapons capability.

During Trump's presentation to Kim, he showed him the outcome of the US's positive trade relations with South Korea, and how they were economically thriving. As I'm sure you are aware, North Korean citizens are starving and very poor and have been for decades. During the 1990s there were rumors of cannibalism in certain communities within the broken nation. Only the people in power had money and lived fruitful lives, as in all communist nations.

I remember seeing Propaganda Village, as the West called it, from the fence line on the DMZ. It was a small town of nice buildings, with people walking around. It happened to be vacant, placed there only for the South and the Americans to see. In the 1970s, an American soldier actually defected to the North after being bribed with millions of dollars for him and his family—part of the propaganda streaming over the loudspeakers that I told you about earlier. His family received pieces of his body in the mail.

Let me get back to the Singapore Summit. During his presentation, Trump, along with Secretary of State Pompeo, enticed Kim with mockup pictures of a North Korean shoreline with condominiums and hotels. Trump told Kim that North Korea could someday be a vacation spot for eastern Asia. I remember only seeing bits and pieces of the presentation on the news, but if you have ever been to the Korean Peninsula, the doctored images definitely looked like hope compared to how it looks today, especially from the North Korean leader's eyes, I'm sure.

The two leaders signed an agreement that offered hope for positive negotiations and more promises from Kim. Back home, the left was losing it. The media reported that Donald Trump had gone overboard in negotiations with a communist dictator. The only request Kim had that President Trump agreed to was to stop the annual combined training exercises between the US and South Korean Army. Trump wasn't a big fan of it anyway because of the hundreds of millions of dollars it cost every year. I remember the president complaining that the Air Force and Navy aircraft used in the training exercises would come all the way from Guam and then fly back. You're talking millions of dollars in fuel alone. I remember that exact exercise when I was stationed there. It was nothing more than a combined arms live-fire exercise. We trained more intensely than that internally within our platoon, company, and battalion, and we did it all the time. I had never spent so much time in the field in my twenty years in the Army.

Anyway, the summit was a success for the United States and the world. Families put to rest loved ones missing in action from the Korean War, missile testing ceased (for that time period), threats to neighboring countries ceased, and captured US citizens were returned home. Donald Trump received zero praise from the left.

Trump's next summit with Kim was in Hanoi, Vietnam, in 2019. That was supposed to be the clincher for North Korea to begin dismantling their nuclear capability with US and UN inspectors ensuring the process was being completed to standard, or at all—not like Iraq years prior, where UN inspectors were being kicked out and prevented from entering Iraq's nuclear facilities.

This summit unfortunately did not have a positive ending. President Trump actually turned down Kim Jong-un's offer, ended the summit, and walked out. Hey, man, look who we're talking about—Donald Trump. The man's been doing this his entire adult life, and even wrote two books about it! He is not going to be intimidated or pressured to "make a deal" that's not good for the United States simply for political reasons. He's not that guy, and he proved it. Chairman Kim went back to North Korea via train. He was not a happy camper. The left and media, if I recall correctly, didn't have much to say about this negative turnout. I mean, what could they say? That the president walked away from a poor deal with a communist leader?

A couple of months later, President Trump met with Kim Jong-un again. This time it was after Trump's visit with the South Korean president Moon Jae-in, and it took place in the DMZ, in Panmunjom, where the 1953 Korean Armistice Agreement was signed. This is the most intense area of the DMZ. The buildings are right on the line of demarcation, and an actual line on the table separates North from South Korea. That's how serious that shit is over there. Both South and North Korean soldiers stand firm, they do not move, do not speak to their counterparts, but simply stare each other down. They do this for hours at a time.

President Trump met with Kim there and negotiated about his nuclear weapons for a fifty-minute period. When they were done, they both walked out, and Kim escorted Trump across the line of demarcation on the DMZ, into North Korea. The two shook hands and walked back to the other side of the southern border. President Trump is the only US president to ever meet with a leader of North Korea, and is the first US president to officially step foot into North Korea itself. The Democrats in Congress, especially Chuck Schumer and Nancy Pelosi, along with the media, called it a cheap photo-op. God forbid they ever gave him props for accomplishing historical events such as meeting, negotiating for peace, and walking across the DMZ with the leader of one of the most brutal communist regimes on the planet. By this time, everyone in the country, especially us Trump supporters, had realized that he was damned if he did and damned if he didn't. If the man cured cancer, he would be criticized for putting pharmaceutical companies out of business.

President Donald Trump with Chairman Kim Jong-un

The replacement of the Affordable Care Act was probably the only promise that President Trump could not deliver on, even with a Senate and House majority. Yes, there were Republican senators who wanted President Trump to fail just as much as the Democrats did. They are referred to as "never Trumpers." The bill went pretty smoothly in the House of Representatives—with some changes at the negotiating table by the Democrats, of course. That fight is pretty much always to be expected: "You want this, so give us that." The Health

Care Freedom Act, also known as the "skinny repeal," got passed in the House. However, then it got to the Senate, which had only a slim majority of Republicans—I believe the count was fifty-one to forty-nine. Susan Collins, Lisa Murkowski, and, lo and behold, Trump's twenty-year opposition John McCain voted nay. The Affordable Care Act stays in effect to this day, but without the IRS penalty.

John McCain died August 25, 2018, of brain cancer. Although President Trump did not attend his memorial services on Capitol Hill, he gave a formal statement of his condolences for his service to our country, and ordered all flags nationwide, including at the White House, to be flown at half-mast in his memory. Shortly after, Senator McCain's daughter left Fox News to work as the conservative voice on *The View.*

President Trump's signature campaign promise was that the United States would have a wall built along our southern border. By the time he was ready to implement his plan in the House of Representatives, the majority was still with the Republicans, though he would have to negotiate with then minority leader Nancy Pelosi in order to get her caucus's support. The Republicans still had the majority of the Senate as well, but he would again need Democrat support because the bill needed sixty votes to pass the Senate. I swear, I learned so much about how our government works in the past four years—more than I ever learned in school, and that includes college.

Trump once said that negotiating with foreign leaders was easier than negotiating with Pelosi. President Trump proposed to Pelosi a path to citizenship for an estimated 1.8 million young, undocumented immigrants in exchange for serious steps to increase our southern border security. This included an approximate eighteen-billion-dollar budget to begin construction of a new border wall. This portion of this chapter and this book is significant to me because the subject of Trump and his hard stance against illegal immigration is probably the main ingredient that separated me from my mother and father. I will explain in a bit, so bear with me.

Trump had already signed an order at the beginning of his presidency to fix many miles of broken and old fencing along parts of California's border with Mexico. However, he was going to need the funding approved by Congress to complete at least five or six hundred miles. He had already been down there and met with the leadership of our border patrol, and was briefed by them on areas that needed a wall and areas that would obviously not require it because of the natural difficult terrain.

The president knew that he wasn't going to get the budget approved for such a project by itself. Every Democrat across the country had been fighting him on the idea of the wall since he announced in 2015 that he was running for president. Why would the same Democrats who voted for border fencing just a few years prior not want a wall for more border security today? The answer is obvious and simple—because it was Donald Trump proposing it, and they believed they had to fight him on it and anything else he promised America, every step of the way. Therefore, he knew he would have to negotiate with Nancy and Chuck for the "dreamers" under DACA, or the Deferred Action for Childhood Arrivals policy that the Democrats had been fighting for and politicizing the entire time Trump was in office.

The DACA program was an executive order signed by President Obama years prior that wasn't even constitutional. Hell, even Obama admitted it wasn't, but he up and did it anyway. President Trump terminated the program that previous September but was going to offer them a swift path to citizenship with this plan he was offering Congress. His terminating the DACA policy not only pissed off the Democrats but earned blowback from some House and Senate Republicans too. Oh yeah, the Congressional Hispanic Caucus was really pissed off.

Trump's plan offered a citizenship path to more than twice as many dreamers enrolled in DACA. Twice as many dreamers! I remember saying to my wife that was a win-win scenario for both parties. The Democrats would get their dreamers citizenship, and in exchange, President Trump would get the budget for the wall construction. I and sixty-three million other Americans were very optimistic and hopeful that this deal would work. I was honestly excited.

The negotiations with Pelosi and Schumer were an utter failure. I couldn't believe it—they turned down his proposal. Actually, I could believe it. They turned down the proposal for the dreamers in order to cause Trump and his base a major loss. They were bound and determined to never allow a border wall, and they proved at the conclusion of their negotiations that they didn't give two shits about the dreamers.

I remember Nancy and Chuck were live on television with Trump in the White House, and Nancy immediately attacked and began to "sharpshoot" him in front of the cameras. She said shit like "You have the majority of the House and Senate, Mr. President, so make it happen."

Trump would remind her and the viewers that he needed sixty votes in the Senate. "You know that, Nancy. You're just playing a game for the cameras." It was something to that effect.

Chuck would come at him with comments such as "You couldn't even get your healthcare bill passed with the majority." Again, Trump had to remind him he needed sixty Senate votes. They were both playing their games, as they did every time they met with him. They would immediately run to the cameras and tell the American people what a bad person he was, and that he wasn't fit for office. That's okay, because in turn, Trump would also go directly to the American people, usually via tweet or a White House briefing to reporters. Of course, they treated him the same way the Democrat leadership would—with disrespect and sarcasm, especially Jim Acosta from CNN.

A federal judge allowed the dreamers to remain in the country; by now, they were mostly adults with careers. Many of them were also in the military, working their way towards citizenship anyway. So, although the DACA program was terminated, the dreamers remained for the most part. Furthermore, the president truly didn't want them to leave the country. He himself even admitted and acknowledged that the US is the only home they've known most of their lives, and it would be an injustice to deport them. Although the left continued throughout his entire presidency to paint a picture of him having no compassion whatsoever, he truly was a man with compassion and courtesy.

After a political struggle for funding, including a thirty-five-day government shutdown that the Dems blamed on Trump, he declared a national emergency. At the end of the day, he was not going to get any assistance on the wall from Congress. He had to find another legal route to fulfil his signature campaign promise. He did sign Executive Order 13767 in the beginning of his presidency, directing the US government to begin wall construction by using existing federal funding approved years prior. After the emergency declaration, he would legally get his funding for 450 to 500 miles of new wall from the Department of Defense budget. Three and a half billion dollars, to be exact.

The government contracted the beginning of construction, and in September 2019, the new wall began going up. By the end of President Trump's time in office, 452 miles of wall had been constructed along our southern border. The argument between the two parties seemed to end, and the country never heard too much about the wall again. Every now and then, the president flew down to inspect the progress. Trump even went a step further and made a deal with Mexico that all foreigners seeking asylum in the United States who came up through Mexico would be held there until their asylum trial came up. For the year 2020, illegal crossings into our southern border decreased by 80 percent. This was a record for the history books.

So, how did Trump's immigration policy hurt my relationship with my family back in Michigan? As most of you are very aware, Facebook and social media as a whole will destroy relationships between friends and families really quick. I will not spend too much time with this, since it is personal, but I believe it necessary for the premise of this book.

I am half Mexican and half White, to start with. Yes, Aguinaga is Spanish, not Japanese as some have misunderstood in the past (I am giggling writing this line). My dad's family came up from Mexico towards the end of WWII. They came with work visas to work in the vegetable fields in Michigan—hence how Michigan was my home state growing up. Remember I told you that my family were dead-set Democrats, right? So, my mother, brother, aunts, and uncles, along with a cousin or two, would disagree with me about the Dems and the GOP quite often. Sometimes these disagreements got heated. At times we went for months without speaking to each other.

The final argument that caused our family breakup was about DACA. One of my cousins asked me what DACA stood for, and I told her. Well, my mother soon arrived to the conversation to throw in her two cents. To make a long story short, my mom and I got into an argument about illegal immigration when she tried to compare our Mexican side of the family's situation to the issues of the southern border crises. I told her to stop comparing our family, who were all here legally and were documented with the government, to illegal aliens who were criminals for crossing the border illegally in the first place. The argument escalated from there, turning to personal attacks. My mom unfriended me, blocked me, and even blocked my calls on her landline. I haven't spoken to my parents or my brother in four years. Like *Forrest Gump* said, "That's all I have to say about that."

President Trump had also promised the American people that he would stop other nations from taking advantage of the United States financially, such as countries in Europe, South Korea, Japan, Mexico, Canada, and most of all China. Trump campaigned on the point that most of these countries were screwing us on trade and money. Let's not forget about how the rest of NATO countries were taking advantage of our funding and military commitments compared to theirs. President Trump let them know very quickly that those days were at an end, and that they would have to step it up with more funding, which they did—another accomplishment that isn't talked about by the Dems at all. Don't worry; us Trump supporters noticed, especially those of us who served in the Armed Forces and saw firsthand how other NATO forces were getting over compared to what our missions were. My wife, who was in the Army and deployed to Kosovo, used to tell me about how the British military had smaller elements over there compared to US forces. Furthermore, the French Army had a total of four firefighters on Camp Able Sentry in Macedonia.

The China Trade Deal was another potential accomplishment that went in the right direction at first. It was a two-part deal with the first portion being signed by both President Trump and President Xi Jinping, who was the general secretary of the Communist Party of China and paramount leader of China. The negotiations went on for months, with both presidents visiting each other during the process. One of the most memorable visits was President Xi's to the White House when President Trump ordered the bombing in Syria on an airbase that launched chemical weapons on Syrian rebels who stood against the army of President Bashar al-Assad. Trump had officially warned them that if the president used chemical weapons on his citizens, the United States would react militarily. It was Donald Trump's "red line." Unlike President Obama, who drew the same red line with Assad years prior after his first chemical attack on the Syrian people, President Trump kept his promise and pretty much destroyed an entire airstrip and hanger.

This act showed not only China but the rest of the world that this president was not fucking around, and would keep his word against aggression across the globe.

While the negotiations occurred between Trump and Xi, Trump had already ordered tariffs on China that were beginning to cripple the communist nation's economy. The first part of the deal was complete; Trump was patiently waiting for part two to get signed. He gave Xi deadlines. Either China got moving on their part, or he would continue to increase the percentage of their tariffs, and he did. By the end of 2019, China's economy was crumbling and fast, while the US was bringing in billions off the trade war as it continued to escalate. Trump would not give in to China or the gutless politicians of "the swamp." After all, China was screwing the United States, making hundreds of billions of dollars every year from unfair trade policies

No president in US history has been as tough on China as President Trump. That's a fact. However, all bets were off with the deal after China unleashed the COVID-19 pandemic on the world in the beginning of 2020. I'll leave that alone for now, as I go into more detail on the subject of COVID-19 in the next chapter. I do have my theories on why China hid this killer disease from the United States and the world, as I probably pretty much just explained in the past couple of paragraphs. It's a shame, too, because this deal would have benefited not only the United States but them as well, the difference being that it would have been a fair deal for both sides instead of only benefiting one.

President Trump once asked President Xi why they had been basically screwing us for decades, how they had gotten away with it for many years, and how it continued. Xi responded that no US president ever tried to stop them, so they kept on "testing the waters" with US leadership. Trump actually admitted that he thought it was a truly honest answer.

President Trump with President Xi Jinping
during their trade negotiations

ISIS was about to be obliterated under the Trump administration. The president called in all chiefs of the military branches and ordered them to wipe out ISIS in the fastest way possible. This was "music to their ears" because what Trump did immediately coming into office was take the handcuffs off the military leadership in order to defeat these monsters on the battlefield. What exactly do I mean by taking off the handcuffs? Well, it's pretty simple. When I was in Iraq in 2003 to 2004, we could fight the enemy without worrying about losing our positions or jobs. Fighting the enemy is not politically correct and never should be. War is war and is brutal and deadly. The Obama administration took that lethal mentality away from the leadership fighting over there.

When I deployed to Iraq in late 2008 to late 2009, our soldiers seemed almost afraid to pull the trigger on the enemies we were there to fight. Back then, it was mostly Al Qaeda in Iraq, or what we in the military referred to as AQI. AQI was basically how ISIS was formed—by their leader, Abu Bakr al-Baghdadi. He was an Iraqi terrorist and the founder of ISIS after AQI's defeat in Baghdad during the US-led surge in 2007, when President Bush ordered an additional 40,000 troops to defeat Al Qaeda in Iraq before it took complete control of Iraq's capital. During that time, deployment of American troops increased from twelve months to fifteen months. After that difficult year of fighting, Coalition Forces won the battle with AQI and order was brought back to the Iraqi government.

Baghdadi took his remaining forces over to Syria and remained silent but was rebuilding a new terrorist organization over the next five to six years. President Bush warned Congress about the consequences if the United States completely withdrew from Iraq and left Al Qaeda to take over the government; a new and more lethal terrorist organization would eventually rise, and that is exactly what happened after the US military withdrawal ordered by President Obama and organized by Vice President Biden in 2011.

During his campaign, President Trump consistently admitted that he was against American forces going into Iraq in the beginning of 2003. As I mentioned earlier, I knew it was coming when I watched Saddam Hussein celebrate the 9/11 attacks on the United States.

Either way, the withdrawal of 100 percent of US forces in 2011 was a perfect recipe for a major terrorist organization such as ISIS to be created. The general officers pleaded with the Obama administration not to withdraw, but because of political reasons and promises he made during his campaign, he did it anyway. The military leaders recommended to leave at least 5,000 troops as a contingency in the event another terrorist situation emerged. I mean, for Christ's sake, we left almost a hundred thousand troops for decades in Europe after WWII, and thousands more in Korea and Japan after the Korean War as well. Why would you not leave at least a combat brigade–level force in the heart of the Middle East? But it was political on the part of the Barrack Obama presidency, and the world paid the price for it.

Here comes the forty-fifth president, left with the heavy burden of removing ISIS from the face of our planet, which he did, and very quickly. Like I alluded to earlier, the first thing he did was give free rein to the commanders in the field. People really need to understand what the role of the military is. It's not to be fair or to coddle its service members in an equal-opportunity environment sensitive to gender preference. It is to kill our enemies—period. President Trump understood that, and shifted the mentality of senior leadership back to that specific concept, especially when it came to defeating ISIS.

I have to give a shoutout to my old friend and commander Captain J from my first book, *Division: Life on Ardennes Street*. He eventually got promoted and became Lieutenant Colonel J and was the battalion commander of the same battalion where he and I served in the 82nd Airborne Division. He deployed that battalion to Iraq to fight ISIS. I just had to throw that out there. It's such a small world and a small Army.

One of the best moves Trump ever made when it came to military leadership was to appoint General Mark A. Milley to be the Chairman of the Joint Chiefs of Staff, which is the top military position for any active duty service member. Colin Powell held this position during the Gulf War. To be honest with you, President Trump raising him to this position in our military was personal for me because I served with and for this man for a year on the DMZ in Korea from 1997 to 1998. He was my battalion commander, ranked as lieutenant colonel at the time.

Man, that dude was fucking tough, and I guarantee he still is today. He was a no-bullshit commander. I mentioned him in my first book *Division: Life on Ardennes Street*, without saying his name, but we all know who this man is today. He fired my first sergeant, and I literally hid behind a copier to witness it. It was the harshest ass-chewing I ever witnessed during my entire twenty years in the military. General Milley was the hardest battalion commander I served with and under, and he was a primary reason why the United States abolished ISIS so quickly, I guarantee it.

Under President Trump's leadership, the United States defeated the Islamic State terrorists very swiftly and with minimal casualties. American forces in Syria had one job, which was to create the right conditions for stability in that region of the world. They accomplished that in a year. President Trump made it abundantly clear that his administration was not interested in "endless wars" or permanently occupying nations all over the world. It's funny when you think about it. Donald Trump's message is exactly what the Dems have been screaming about since the Vietnam era, but when he says it, it's "irresponsible" on his part. Give me a fucking break, ladies and gentlemen—please.

So, back in the day, when I was a young soldier, we used to go to war and defeat our enemies and bring our troops home immediately. Think about it. Grenada—we deployed our military and conquered and came home. Panama—we deployed our military and conquered and came home. Same with Operation Desert Storm. There was a time when we would go and kick ass and bring our troops and their equipment home immediately. When the United States got involved in the Global War on Terrorism, leadership in Washington, DC, kept us there for almost twenty years. When President Trump campaigned and said we needed to pull out of these endless wars in the Middle East, he was immediately labeled by the left as irresponsible. Talk about hypocrisy from Pelosi and Schumer.

When the Coalition Forces led by the United States defeated the caliphate in the Middle East, President Trump ordered our troops to begin withdrawal from Syria and Iraq. He ordered the troop withdrawal from the Syrian and Turkish border after Turkish government officials threatened Syrian forces in that region. Understandably, President Trump said that the United States was not going to get involved in border disputes in the Middle East that have been going on for centuries. Our mission was to take out and defeat ISIS in that region, and we did just that.

The left again lost their minds. Democratic congressmen and women accused the president of withdrawing our troops irresponsibly because Turkey was our ally and part of NATO. President Trump did not fall for their bullshit, and publicly stated that we were not in Syria to stay in their border wars with neighboring countries. We withdrew from Syria, except for a small force to guard and protect the oil refineries in the southern portion of the country. We also left approximately 5,000 troops in Iraq as a contingency if ISIS emerged again someday, which they probably will. Most importantly, if ISIS does begin to rebuild in any part of the Middle East, the US is perfectly capable of responding to their threat with the same deadly force we used to kick their ass in the first place. Does that make sense?

The problem was that the "DC swamp" wanted to leave troops in the Middle East continuously, and President Trump wasn't having it. Wow! A US president who actually kept his promises to the American people. We could get back to going over to any nation if need be, kicking their asses, and bringing our troops home afterwards. We don't have to nation build afterwards, especially when these countries hate us and hate what we stand for. Trump actually understood that concept. So did the previous administrations, but they were more concerned about being "globalists" and did not have the "America first" mentality.

On the evening of October 26, 2019, the United States launched Operation Kayla Mueller, which was a US Delta Force mission to take out Al-Baghdadi in Syria. The elite US counterterrorist organization was to fly in on helicopters launched from their base in Iraq, fly under the radar into Syria, and kill or capture Baghdadi. The mission was successful, with no US personnel wounded or killed, except for one of their military-trained dogs that went after Baghdadi himself in a tunnel. The terrorist killed himself along with two children when he detonated a suicide belt while he was running away from the elite US soldiers. Later, President Trump awarded the dog a medal for bravery. The dog, Conan, was obsessed with Vice President Pence during this presentation.

So, the United States Army Delta Force—or, as the Army officially calls them, Special Forces Operations Detachment Delta—are known throughout the Army and the military as a whole as the baddest of badasses. They are the military's premier counterterrorist organization. Yeah, I know, everyone says the Navy Seal teams are the top dogs, but it comes down to Army Delta Force. Why do you think you don't hear anything about them on television like you do Navy Seal Team members? They can't show their faces, either. In truth, in combat, usually a couple teams of Seals, a couple teams of Army Delta, and a company of Army Rangers for security make up a task force designated for missions throughout the area of operations.

When I lived a short period of time with CPT J before I left Fort Bragg, he had another friend and roommate living in his house with us. He was an "unconfirmed" Delta Force operator. I will not even give him an abbreviation or initial for his name. He was a cool dude, and he and I became friends. One night he and I were working on a bottle of Yukon Jack, and I asked him if he could tell me something about being in the environment of Delta. He said no. I said, "C'mon, man, tell me something." He continued to tell me no. After asking him

again, he finally gave in by simply telling me that he had parachuted
out of a 747 civilian airplane once at 30,000 feet. That means he
had to have an oxygen mask, and the whole nine yards. I remember
asking him where. He replied, "Nice try; change the subject." I did.

The operation to get Baghdadi was named after Kayla Jean Mueller,
a US citizen murdered by ISIS in 2015. She was a human rights activist
and humanitarian aid worker from Arizona. She was taken captive by
ISIS in 2013 in Syria, after leaving a Doctors Without Borders hospital.
She was tortured, raped, and murdered at age twenty-six. Many have
reported that Baghdadi himself brutally and repeatedly raped this
young girl himself. US Army Delta Force prevented this animal from
ever doing this again to another human being. CNN and MSNBC
referred to Baghdadi as a "scholar" and "a leader of a cause." President
Trump honored Kayla and her family during his following State of the
Union speech. Very few Democrats stood and applauded.

President Trump and his staff, including General Mark Milley,
witnessing the raid to kill the ISIS leader Baghdadi, live in real time,
in 2019 at the White House

On January 3, 2020, President Trump ordered an airstrike near
Baghdad International Airport to take out General Qassem Soleimani,
who for years was the Kata'ib Hezbollah terrorist group leader. With

him was Jamal Jaafar-Ibrahim, also known as Abu Mahdi al-Mohandes. He was the head and second in charge of the Quds Force, which was run by Soleimani. The Quds Force's mission is to eventually take back Jerusalem from Israeli control. Meanwhile, this organization's primary mission in the Middle East is to spearhead the export of Iran's Islamic revolution throughout the region and to coordinate the activities of loyal terrorist proxies and militias that Iran has cultivated in countries such as Yemen, Syria, and Iraq.

The terrorist group from Iran, Hezbollah, under complete control of General Soleimani, was responsible for creating and utilizing the deadly explosively formed penetrator, or the EFP. The EFP was an improvised explosive device, or a roadside bomb, commonly used by the Iranians against US-led Coalition Forces in Iraq throughout the latter days of Operation Iraqi Freedom. These new IEDs could penetrate straight through any armored US vehicle. Soleimani had hundreds of US service members' blood on his hands. In my book *Wake Up, You're Having Another Nightmare*, I talk about this in detail because two soldiers in our battalion lost their legs to EFP strikes.

President Trump had an intelligence report straight from the Pentagon that US Special Operation Forces had direct "eyes-on" the target—Soleimani himself, and his lieutenant. President Trump ordered his death on the spot, without hesitation, and our forces once again followed through. The military refers to these individuals as "targets." I refer to them as pieces of shit. President Trump was again applauded by his supporters for taking out a high-value target. The Democrats and their left-wing base on CNN and MSNBC referred to this incident as a "US assassination of a foreign leader." Iran has vowed revenge for his death.

Now, you have to remember, while the Trump administration was accomplishing these things, he was under a two-and-a-half-year investigation for supposedly colluding and conspiring with the Russian government to win the 2016 presidential election against Hillary Clinton. I swear to God, if I heard the term *collusion* one more time between 2017 and 2018, I was going to throw up—seriously.

Operation Crossfire Hurricane was the code name for the counterintelligence investigation undertaken by the Federal Bureau of Investigation from July 2016 to May 2017. So, this basically began immediately after Donald Trump was announced as the Republican Party's primary candidate. Led by James Comey, the director of the FBI, and his assistant, Andrew McCabe, Crossfire Hurricane was supposed to discover links between Trump associates and Russian officials and determine whether individuals associated with Donald Trump's presidential campaign coordinated, wittingly or unwittingly, with the Russian government's efforts to interfere in the 2016 election. Give me a fucking break. Really? Again, the American people could see through this bullshit investigation from the very beginning. Trump had joked at one of his numerous rallies, saying something to the effect of "Hey, Russia, help us out please. Can you find Crooked Hillary's thirty-three thousand emails please?" The left took it and ran with it, immediately crying conspiracy.

The investigation went on during the campaign but didn't evolve into a full-blown Department of Justice investigation until after Trump was sworn into office as the forty-fifth president of the United States. It then turned into the "Robert Mueller Investigation," and the whole country would have to wait years to hear what we already knew. That the Russian government did not collude with the Trump campaign in any way, shape, or form. This entire idea was the Democrats', led by Nancy Pelosi and of course Adam Schiff, the chairman of the House of Representatives Permanent Select Committee on Intelligence. Adam Schiff—or as Trump had already nicknamed him, "Shifty Schiff"—went before the news cameras numerous times a week, saying that he had solid evidence of the Trump campaign colluding with the Russian government.

The Foreign Intelligence Surveillance Act, or FISA, was initiated by a court of eleven judges in 1978 in order to oversee requests for surveillance warrants against foreign spies inside the United States by federal law enforcement and intelligence agencies. A FISA warrant was authorized and given to then FBI agent Christopher Steele, who led up the investigation on Donald Trump's campaign. How did he obtain such a specific and difficult warrant from the FISA Court, one might ask? Simple. He obtained a fake dossier on Donald Trump from a British reporter—some call him an intelligence agent (who really knows)—who was paid for by the Hillary Clinton campaign.

In March 2019, after about twenty-two million taxpayer dollars had been spent, special counsel Robert Mueller's probe into Russian meddling in the 2016 election came to an end. The investigation, or as President Trump continued to call it for the entire two and a half years, the "witch hunt," found zero evidence that the president's campaign colluded with Russia but fell short of completely exonerating the president. Go figure. Again, a flat-out lie to the American people, and the entire world as well.

Christopher Steele was under congressional investigations and during the hearings admitted that he was a former MI-6 agent from Great Britain. Follow me now: He admitted to not wanting Donald Trump to win because he didn't want him to hurt relations between the United States and Great Britain. There is still an ongoing criminal investigation by the Department of Justice under a man named John Durham on all these matters. We are still waiting on his report to Congress. Will we ever receive it? Who knows? Probably not, since as I am writing this, we are well over a hundred days into the Biden administration.

The VA Mission Act was signed into law by President Trump in 2018. He also referred to it as the "Right to Choose Act." This new law gave more veterans access to private health care that would in turn be paid for by the VA. Let me give you a personal example of how this affected me as a veteran who has been part of the VA system since I retired from the Army eleven years ago.

During the previous administration, if I had a medical emergency, I would have to drive from my home here in Northwest Ohio all the way up to the VA hospital in Ann Arbor, Michigan. That is about an hour-and-fifteen-minute drive from my home. Although I am assigned to the Toledo VA Clinic, which is about a forty-mile drive for me, Ann Arbor is the headquarters VA of Toledo. So, in order to go to a medical emergency room through the VA, I would have to drive up to the actual hospital. To be completely honest with you, since I am retired military, I also receive Tricare Health Insurance but would have a hell of a copay, which increased throughout the years thanks to Obamacare. The VA healthcare system for me is free, due to me being 90 percent permanently disabled.

With the new VA Mission Act, I can go to my local county hospital for emergency care or any other medical procedure if need be, and the VA will cover it 100 percent. I still have to call the Ann Arbor VA emergency section and tell them my medical issue and why I may need emergency care so they can approve the emergency room visit, but the bottom line is that I no longer have to drive almost seventy-five miles; I only have to go ten miles north or south of where I live.

To back up a little bit, in 2017 President Trump passed the VA Accountability and Whistleblower Protection Act. This new law gave the management of these VA clinics and hospitals the right to basically fire any employees who were substandard or treated the veterans disrespectfully, which was a regular occurrence when I first got into their system. To get rid of government employees back in the day was virtually impossible.

Just to give you another personal example of this subject from my experiences with the VA, and trust me, I have plenty, last year in the Ann Arbor VA, I had to get my blood drawn. After seeing my doctor for my appointment, my last medical station was the lab station. When you have to travel the distance that I did, the VA gives you travel pay and it is direct-deposited into your bank account. So, when I was complete with my lab draws, it was time for me to check out and go back home to Ohio.

The lady behind the counter asked me what I needed. I told her I was complete with all my appointments and that I simply needed to do my travel pay. She sarcastically told me that I needed to go back to the doctor's office where my last medical station was. I told her that *this was my last station*. Seriously, all you have to do to get travel pay these days is swipe your VA ID card through the electronic device she had at her station. The truth of the matter was that I had interrupted whatever she was doing on her computer, and she was irritated with me.

I told her, "Never mind, I'm sorry to have interrupted whatever it is you're doing on your computer. Have a nice day." She got my irritation vibe, and immediately called me back: "Sir, sir, I can help you." She knew I was pissed off. After two or three hours in that fucking place, my mentality was "They can keep their fucking sixty-five dollars travel pay—fuck 'em." I just wanted to get out of there and go home. I could have turned her in for not wanting to help me or do her job, but I let it go because I had been there long enough.

President Trump signed into law the Right to Try Act in May 2018. This law gives patients who have been diagnosed with life-threatening diseases or conditions, have tried all approved treatment options, and are unable to participate in a clinical trial access to certain non-FDA-approved treatments. This was a large accomplishment and chance for hope for critically ill Americans, especially for cancer and AIDS patients. However, the left once again shit all over it, or simply didn't acknowledge it at all.

Greg Gutfeld from the Fox News Channel once said on *The Five*, "If Donald Trump is a racist, he sure sucks at it. He is the worst racist in US history." To reiterate, President Trump was never labeled with such a disgusting phrase until he won the GOP primaries.

Alice Johnson is an African American woman and former federal prisoner who is now an advocate for prison reform. She spent twenty years behind bars before President Trump granted her clemency in 2018—or, simply put, ordered her out of prison. From Mississippi, Alice Johnson was sixty-five years old and had spent two decades in prison for a nonviolent crime. In 1996, Johnson was sentenced to life imprisonment without parole for her involvement in a Memphis cocaine-trafficking gang. She was unemployed at the time and recently divorced when she became a "telephone mule," relaying messages between drug distributors and sellers. She was charged and sentenced to the harshest sentence—a sentence that murder-one felons receive. Her crime was conspiracy to possess cocaine and attempted possession of cocaine and money laundering.

Kim Kardashian fought to have Ms. Johnson freed after hearing about her case. She lobbied for her released in a high-profile campaign alongside her husband Kanye West, who at the time had become an advocate and supporter of President Trump. Kim and Kanye both approached the president and conveyed to him the injustice of Ms. Johnson's case. President Trump granted this woman clemency a week after he met with Kim and Kanye. President Obama had denied her clemency in 2016.

President Trump granted Alice Johnson, a former federal prisoner, a full pardon in June 2018

That same year, President Trump signed into law the First Step Act, which also reauthorized the Second Chance Act. This built on and strengthened the landmark legislation originally passed ten years prior. The Second Chance Reauthorization Act of 2018, which was sponsored by Senators Portman from Ohio and Leahy from Vermont, provides one hundred million per year to establish and enhance state and local programs that promote successful reentry for people returning to their communities after being released from prison. Many of these ex-convicts are nonviolent offenders guilty of drug charges, and many are minority races and first-time offenders like Alice Johnson. Fifteen or twenty years ago, most people released from prison would have difficulty finding jobs or starting a career due to their criminal records. Many of them would be lucky to find work at Walmart or a fast food restaurant.

The Second Chance Act also expands efforts to reduce drug addiction among people in the justice system. At a time when our nation is confronted with a growing number of people with emotional, mental, and behavioral health needs within our prison system, correctional and reentry programs provide important services and support to address these needs and prevent future contact with the criminal justice system. In addition, the act establishes priority consideration for nonprofit organizations that have formed partnerships with state and local establishments to develop programs that treat substance addiction in the prisoner reentry population, as well as grants to residential substance-addiction programs and family supportive services in correctional facilities.

During President Trump's last week in office, he pardoned 143 people who received last-minute clemency. Most of them were imprisoned for nonviolent drug crimes, and many of those were elderly, such as Ms. Johnson.

I believe some other major accomplishments of President Trump's first three years in office should and will go down in history. Almost four million jobs have been created since 2016; pre-coronavirus, more

Americans were employed than at any other time in history. More than 400,000 manufacturing jobs existed, growing at the fastest pace in over three decades. Economic growth hit 4.2 percent at one point. During the Hillary and Trump campaigns of 2016, Barrack Obama said that manufacturing jobs were gone and never coming back, claiming that Donald Trump would have to wave a "magic wand" to get these jobs back. Like I said earlier, Trump was succeeding as president-elect before he was even sworn into office.

By 2019, the unemployment claims across our nation hit a fifty-year record low. The median household income was the highest ever recorded in US history. African American, Hispanic American, and Asian American unemployment rates were also at their lowest in history. Again, if Donald Trump is a racist, he must be the worst racist in US history. The left and especially CNN, MSNBC, and shows like *The View* continuously referred to him as a racist and a Nazi. Are you fucking kidding me? Do these people truly know or understand what it means to be a Nazi?

To be "a Nazi," first and foremost, you have to hate one major particular group of people—the Jewish community. I think we can all agree with that fact, right? President Trump had probably, in my lifetime, one of the best relationships with Israel of any sitting US president. He moved the US embassy from Tel Aviv, which was Palestinian territory, to Jerusalem. This was a campaign promise made by many US presidents throughout history, but President Trump was the one to come through. The left lost their minds again, saying that this would bring additional war in the area, which never happened. If Donald Trump was a Nazi, he was the worst Nazi ever. For Christ's sake, he has a Jewish son-in-law, and a grandchild being raised in the Jewish tradition. His daughter even converted to Judaism.

My wife just scolded me for saying "Christ's sake" while discussing the subject of Trump being a Jewish religion supporter. She said, "Nate, I don't think putting 'for Christ's sake' is a good term when talking and defending any religion, as we are both Catholic." She laughed at me, and I had to throw that in this book for you. Every now and then I write a paragraph or page and read it back to my wife. Of course, she always gives me her critique as a spouse.

Women's unemployment reached the lowest rate in sixty-five years. I remember Trump used to apologize for the rate not being the lowest in US history as it was for African, Asian, and Hispanic Americans. He used to say to the women in his crowds, "Don't worry, ladies, we'll get there." Youth unemployment reached the lowest rate in nearly half a century, as did unemployment for Americans without high school diplomas.

Veteran unemployment reached its lowest rate in nearly twenty years, and almost 3.9 million Americans have left food stamps since 2016. The administration's job-training initiative had employers committing to vocational training more than four million people. Young Americans were no longer being pressured to have a college degree in order to make a living; they were encouraged to seek more vocational education. In high school, I went to vocational training in welding for two years. When I graduated, I immediately got hired at a small welding shop in my town in Michigan. It paid more than minimum wage at that time, and I was proud to have it straight out of high school. Of course, I chose a life in the military and pursued that path instead, which turned out to be a success for me.

His next major accomplishment was in the judicial branch. President Trump nominated three conservative-constitutionalist judges to the Supreme Court. These judges were part of a list he shared during his campaign in 2016. Another promise kept. The most memorable aspect was the scrutinization by the Senate Democrats of Justice Brett Kavanaugh. I watched that hearing live for weeks on Fox News. I couldn't believe what the Dems were doing to this man, who had an impeccable record, not only of law practice as a judge but as a human being and family man as well.

As we all remember, during his Senate hearings on Capitol Hill, he was accused of raping a girl in high school by the Democrat senators.

They had the accuser appear before the Judiciary Committee to testify against Judge Kavanaugh, and she utterly failed to provide believable testimony. She could not remember where, when, or how this rape occurred; she couldn't even remember how she knew Kavanaugh. This happened in front of the American people, live on television. Judge Kavanaugh became the second Supreme Court justice appointed under President Trump. Trump later admitted that several Republican leaders in the White House and in Congress attempted to convince him to let the judge go and choose somebody else. President Trump refused, and fought for him instead.

One of the highest achievements of the Trump administration—which he still never gets credit for, even after the vaccines are getting distributed by the millions—was his creation of Operation Warp Speed. The mission was to produce a vaccine to the COVID-19 virus as quickly as possible, and it did indeed. I will get into this achievement more in the next chapter, but it was referred to as a "medical miracle." The United States produced a vaccine within ten months of the disease reaching our shores; history proves that it would normally take scientists years.

I could write an entire book on President Trump's accomplishments on behalf of the American people. My point in this chapter is that he got these tasks done for us, as promised during his campaign, and accomplished them in his first three years in office.

CHAPTER 5

2020: A YEAR THE ENTIRE WORLD COULD HAVE DONE WITHOUT

At the beginning of 2020 the United States economy was booming, our country was thriving as the scientific and space-research leader of the globe once again, and our military was definitely on top of every other nation on the planet. We had a brand-new branch of our military forces with the new Space Force. I mean, it was on, ladies and gentlemen. I and millions of people in our country saw a nation thriving once again with hope of more improvement. Unemployment and illegal immigration were at historic lows. Law enforcement was being respected again, and finally, world leaders respected the United States of America once again after decades of decline and being taken advantage of financially and militarily. President Trump's ideology and methods returned the United States to its status as the leader of the free world. Other countries may not have liked his demeaner at times, but President Trump was not out to earn friendship and popularity.

How did 2020 begin for our country with all these positive points and the positive direction our country was moving in? Nancy Pelosi led the march in the House of Representatives to impeach President Trump and remove him from office. What perfect timing—the beginning of a presidential election year. At the end of 2019, going into January 2020, President Trump became the third president in America's history to be impeached by the House of Representative. First, there was President Andrew Johnson in the year 1868, then President Bill Clinton in 1998, and third was Trump. For what, you might ask? Over a fucking phone call Trump had in order to congratulate the new president of Ukraine, Volodymyr Zelensky.

It was another "gotcha" moment for Pelosi and Schumer's campaign to rid our nation of this president—as I like to refer to it, the only chance they had to remove President Trump from office. They knew with his record on the economy and overseas accomplishments, their party wouldn't be able to win at the ballot box in November. For two and a half years, they put all their money on the Russian collusion investigation being their ticket to impeach him, but that obviously failed. President Trump was fighting for the American people and not the global industry leaders that helped fund the Democrats' campaigns over the years. His "America first" way of governing our nation was definitely a stone in the Democrats' shoes.

Nancy Pelosi wasted no time in putting together the articles of impeachment for President Trump's phone conversation with the new president of Ukraine. Supposedly a whistleblower heard about it from another source, from a third person sitting in the room with President Trump when he made the phone call. The funny part of this so-called whistleblower was that there were about a dozen other people in the room too, including two or three individuals who were transcribing his entire conversation.

On December 18, 2019, President Trump was officially impeached by the 116th United States Congress. The House of Representative adopted two articles of impeachment against the forty-fifth president: abuse of power and obstruction of Congress.

So, let's get into why the Democrats thought they were going to get him this time in the first place. What was "Nervous Nancy"

Pelosi's and Adam "Shifty" Schiff's reasoning? It was simple. President Trump was asking for assurances from President Zelensky that he would combat the corruption of the Ukraine government, known to be one of the most corrupt governments in Eastern Europe since the end of Soviet domination. President Trump wanted these assurances because the United States was sending Ukraine about four hundred million dollars a year in financial aid, particularly for their military. Let's not forget that when Trump came into office, he authorized supplying the Ukrainian army with US anti-tank weapon systems in order to defend themselves from the Russian forces that invaded their country during the Obama administration; by the way, Russia never suffered any repercussions from the United States. Instead, President Obama sent Ukrainian forces blankets and first-aid items.

So, during President Trump's phone call with the Ukraine leader, he asked if Zelensky would be willing to look into Hillary Clinton's private server. President Trump had received intelligence that her server was said to be kept in Ukraine. He then asked Zelensky to look into Hunter Biden's dealings with Burisma, an energy company. Hunter Biden had zero schooling or training in the energy business, but the son of the then vice president of the United States had received millions of dollars from this company.

The Democrats took that question and ran with it as Donald Trump attempting to get a foreign government to assist him in the upcoming 2020 election, which is illegal. However, President Trump said it had nothing to do with the upcoming election and everything to do with the United States funding a corrupt foreign government. I mean, the guy ran on that promise to the American people. He had said since 2015 that if he were elected president, the days of the United States sending millions of dollars overseas—especially to nations that hate us, such as Pakistan—would be over. He kept his promise. Just because Joe Biden had thrown his hat into running for president didn't mean that his son's crooked dealings were off the table.

At the time, Joe Biden still wasn't the official Democrat candidate. Furthermore, since when is it illegal for a sitting president who is funding a foreign government with taxpayer dollars to ensure that government is not dealing in corruption? And does anybody truly believe that President Trump was at any time worried about having to defeat Joe Biden? I mean seriously. The man couldn't and still cannot put together two complete sentences without screwing his entire point up, but I'll get more into that in the next chapter.

In December 2019, impeachment proceedings began. Representative Adam Schiff headed up the investigation on President Trump—yeah, the crooked politician who lied to our entire country for two and a half years that he had solid evidence of Trump colluding with the Russian government during the Mueller investigation and then didn't produce shit. So, Schiff, who is the chairman of the Intelligence Committee, was running the impeachment process. Usually that is the responsibility of the House Judiciary Committee, but because Jerry Nadler, the chairman of that committee, screwed up and couldn't produce a win for the Democrats during the collusion hoax, Nancy Pelosi let Schiff handle the impeachment proceedings.

Right from the beginning of this bullshit procedure, Representative Schiff lied on record and in front of the American people by making false statements about the conversation between Trump and Zelensky. He faked reading the transcript between the two, making false statements such as "I need you to do me a favor, and I'm going to ask you several times to dig up dirt on Joe Biden for me." I watched it live, yelling at the television that it was bullshit. Frustratingly, no Republican called him out on it. It was all a show from the beginning, ladies and gentlemen. Again, they think the American people are stupid enough to buy it. Quotes from the actual transcript on that portion of their conversation had been released, and I and millions of others knew it.

As soon as Adam "Shifty Schiff" lied during this congressional hearing, live on television, President Trump declassified and released the full transcript to the entire country. Wow! The Dems were completely pissed off because they never expected the president to release this publicly, but he did, and he did it very quickly. It was verified as authentic and comprehensive. It also verified that Adam Schiff's initial report before the nation was false. Not only was he caught in this lie, but the American people could see and had direct access to the entire conversation via Google at the drop of a dime. I know because I printed the damn thing off, and it was literally a five-page, less-than-five-minute conversation. However, this was the anti-Trump movement's best opportunity to remove this man from office.

Officially, Trump's impeachment came after a formal inquiry alleged that he had solicited foreign interference in the 2020 US presidential election to help his reelection bid and then obstructed the inquiry itself by telling his administration officials to ignore subpoenas for documentation and testimony. The Dems' main argument for this was that President Trump withheld the annual payment of four hundred million until Ukrainian officials began their investigation on the Biden family, which also turned out to be false. Trump never mentioned aid withdrawal during the entire phone conversation with Zelensky. When he authorized and demanded the conversation be released to the public, the Dems realized that their quid pro quo accusations were not going to work—not with the Senate trials, and not with the American people.

During the preparation phase for the witnesses testifying before Adam Schiff and the House Intelligence Committee, the majority of them were taken to the SCIF, or the Sensitive Compartmented Information Facility, which is in a secured location in the House. These witnesses were questioned one at a time on their upcoming sworn testimony. Republican representatives were not allowed into the questioning process. Many of them, including Representatives Devin Nunes and Jim Jordan, were convinced it was more of a "grooming stage." I agree.

My favorite and one of the most memorable witnesses was Army lieutenant colonel Alexander Vindman, who provided lawmakers with some of the most damaging testimony during the impeachment proceedings. At least, the Democrats in the House thought it was, but I wasn't buying his shit. He was more of a proxy for the lawmakers and apparently a Trump-hater himself. His title and official duty position in the Pentagon was the National Security Council director for European affairs. He was also a combat veteran of the Global War on Terrorism and had been awarded the Purple Heart.

When I saw his testimony live, he seemed to be going after the president of the United States with full force. I remember asking my wife, "Who is this obviously overweight lieutenant colonel?" I spent twenty years in the same corporation, and there are two standards every soldier must maintain for their entire time in service—they must pass the Army physical fitness test and the Army height and weight standards. I took one look at this guy and knew he could not. Now, I will never bash any man or woman's service to our great nation; I'm simply making a professional observation—one senior leader's perspective of another senior leader. Don't get me wrong, there were a couple times in my military career where I was told to drop weight or else, maybe ten or fifteen pounds here and there. I did and did it quickly. But that was also when I was older.

During the House hearings when Lieutenant Colonel Vindman was making his testimony—which was proving nothing and going nowhere, like those of everyone else testifying on behalf of the Democrats—Pete Hegseth from Fox News made some comments that stuck with me. Pete, who is also a retired field-grade officer from the US Army, said not only what I said about Vindman's weight and physical fitness ability as an active duty soldier but also noted that this man returned to duty the day he was wounded and earned his Purple Heart, and that he was a senior leader in combat but didn't even receive a Bronze Star Medal for service. As a retired active duty member who really understands the military, I realized that perhaps this guy was not everything the Democrats on Capitol Hill made him out to be.

You see, my point is not to criticize this man's service but to highlight to you that the Democrats will criticize and are willing to ruin service member's lives if they are on the same page as Republicans. Does that make sense? Dems had no problem destroying General Petraeus and General Flynn, but when it came to Senator McCain or this Lieutenant Colonel Vindman, they were "war heroes." Especially when it came to Senator McCain, like I told you earlier. It was his status as a Trump-hater, not as a veteran or former POW, that made him a war hero to them. They did the same thing and fawned over Vindman the entire time he was being questioned by the Dems in the House. As a matter of fact, every one of them began with, "I would like to start off by thanking you for your service to our nation" or "Our nation owes you our undying gratitude for your service." Really? They were ready to put General Flynn away for life for being coerced into a lie by the FBI—and the FBI even admitted to doing this.

These hypocrites will make you sick. If you're a senior leader in the military and are against Trump, you're a hero. If you support Trump and his policies, you deserve to be behind bars. That obviously doesn't just go for military or ex-military leaders but ex-cabinet or staff members as well, as we all witnessed—men like Steve Bannon and Roger Stone, just to name two out of numerous others. For Christ's sake, Roger Stone is a senior citizen, age sixty-seven with no prior criminal record or convictions. His home was invaded by a SWAT team in a raid in the middle of the night, with CNN cameras ready to film. Wow, that wasn't tipped off as a political move on behalf of the Dems, right? He was charged with lying to Congress about his communications related to document-disclosure group WikiLeaks.

Now, I've been on raids to capture some pretty bad characters associated with Al Qaeda and other terrorist groups, but I've never seen this much firepower and effort to get an elderly man out of his home in the middle of the night for a nonviolent crime. Anyway, in January 2019, they ripped this nonviolent offender out of society and immediately placed him behind bars, and made sure it was live on CNN. Why would they do this to this man and his wife in the middle of the night? Simply put, he was a longtime friend and an advocate of Donald Trump.

Steve Bannon was an officer in the United States Navy for seven years in the late 1970s and early 1980s. After his military service, he worked for Goldman Sachs as an investment banker for a couple years. He later became a movie producer in Hollywood and produced eighteen movies between 1991 and 2016. In the same year, he became Trump's chief executive officer of his presidential campaign. He was appointed chief strategist and senior counselor to the president following the election. He was fired by Trump eight months later, and in January 2018, he was disavowed by the president for critical comments Bannon made about him in his book *Fire and Fury.*

So, why do I bring up Steve Bannon in this chapter? The same reason I mentioned Roger Stone. He too was arrested, in August 2020, and charged with conspiracy to commit mail fraud and money laundering in connection to the We Build the Wall campaign. The funny part was that he and Trump were talking shit about one another and not talking to each other at all. It was clear to our nation that their friendship had pretty much ended, but the Dems had Bannon arrested and charged anyway. Don't get me wrong—nobody is above the law; just ask Hillary Clinton. However, isn't it ironic that the FBI continued to go after former workers and supporters of Trump, whether they were fired or not? I'm pretty sure they were hoping to get them to turn and bring up dirt on the president in order to get clemency for their crimes. Whatever. It never happened either way.

Getting back to the impeachment hearings of the forty-fifth president, the House Intelligence and Judiciary Committees wrapped up their portion of witnesses, and the next move was to vote whether to impeach Trump on the House floor. Of course, with a Democrat majority, it didn't take a genius to figure out that the vote would go their way. On the first charge of abuse of power, the results were 230 votes in favor and 197 votes against. For the second charge of obstruction of Congress, 229 voted in favor, and 198 voted against.

The next step in this impeachment process was to physically hand over the charges to the US Senate for a trial. This was funny because Senator Lindsay Graham from South Carolina wasn't entertaining it at all. He was the Senate Judiciary chairman and warned the House Democrats that they were not going to even have a trial, due to no weight of evidence of a crime being committed. He called it right from the start—that this was a continuing political witch hunt for a president the Democrats had wanted removed before he was even sworn into office almost four years prior.

Senate majority leader Mitch McConnel stated that they would immediately vote on whether to convict the president on the Senate floor without an actual trial, and they did just that. Basically, the impeachment process was dead on arrival once it hit the Senate. It's funny when you think about it, and I told my wife this throughout his presidency: our Founding Fathers knew it could be a problem in the future if you had a majority in the House that simply wanted to remove a president they did not agree with. The Founding Fathers created another legislative body called the Senate to keep them in check—to maintain a system of checks and balances within our federal government. They called it almost 245 years ago that this could happen; and it has—twice. I say twice because when President Clinton was impeached in the late 1990s, the Republicans had the majority in the House. Although the impeachment charge of lying under oath to Congress was more concrete, it did not equate to a criminal offense worth removal from office. It actually bit the Republicans in the ass, and the House Speaker at the time, Newt Gingrich, admits that to this day. Bill Clinton had over a 70 percent approval rating as he left office a little over a year later. It almost cost the Republicans the 2000 election if you remember the Florida debacle.

The Democrat leadership of the House walked the articles of impeachment to the Senate live on television, like they were some kind of military organization marching in a parade. That's how it appeared to me and my wife, anyway. Anything to get in front of the cameras.

With that, it went to the Republican-led Senate for an immediate vote. In the Senate, to vote to find a president guilty of a crime, and for removal from office, they must have sixty-seven votes. On Article 1—abuse of power—the vote came to forty-eight "guilty" and fifty-two "not guilty." Only one Republican Senator voted "guilty" against the president, and guess who it was? Good old Mitt Romney, who hated Trump from the very beginning, and why? Because Trump called him out for fucking up the 2012 campaign against Barrack Obama. You hate the guy, I got it, but where was he wrong? Trump didn't like Romney because he is a phony career politician, at least in mine and millions of other voters' opinions.

On Article II—obstruction of Congress—there were forty-seven "guilty" votes, and fifty-three "not guilty." The result was that President Trump was acquitted of any legal wrongdoing on February 5, 2020, and remained in office as the president of the United States. Senator Lindsey Graham led that campaign to save the president, along with many other congressmen and women on Capitol Hill, such as Jim Jordan, Devin Nunes, and Senators Ted Cruz, Rand Paul, and Marco Rubio, just to name a few. Mitch McConnel supported Trump at the time as well, but I'll get into his demise later.

Impeachment has become an easy process to remove someone you don't like, without an actual crime or proper court or hearing procedures. "Fuck it! Just get rid of him or her" is the new norm for the Democrats on Capitol Hill. It's like what happens in socialist and communist regimes across the globe. George Orwell wrote two books on this happening to a great nation, which my wife is reading now—*Animal Farm* and *1984*. He wrote both in the late 1940s, and their premise is based on how quickly a government by the people and for the people could move to a communist state. Are we starting to see that now? That's for another book someday.

So, the Democrats in Congress failed for the second time to remove President Trump from office. With the help of the Department of Justice, former FBI leadership under the last administration, so-called whistleblowers, and a two-and-a-half-year investigation under Robert Mueller, they just couldn't get it done. After this second failure to get Trump out of the White House and out of Washington, DC, altogether, it seemed as if they had no way of removing him or preventing him from winning the upcoming election that fall.

Just wait, though; a deadly disease was about to be unleashed on the world.

Senator Lindsey Graham attacking his Democratic colleagues for their attempted character assassination campaign of Judge Kavanaugh during his Senate confirmation hearings. This will go down in history as being one of Graham's most memorable moments during his time on Capitol Hill.

On January 9, 2020, the World Health Organization announced that there was a mysterious coronavirus-related pneumonia in Wuhan, China. By January 20, the Centers of Disease Control and Prevention, or CDC, said that three major US airports would begin screening for coronavirus. Three additional cases of what is now known as

COVID-19 were reported in Thailand and Japan, causing the CDC to begin screenings at JFK International, San Francisco International, and Los Angeles International airports. These were primarily chosen because they had direct flights between Wuhan and the United States. By January 21, the CDC confirmed the first US coronavirus case in Washington state, in an individual who had returned from Wuhan on January 15. On the same day, Chinese scientists confirmed COVID-19 human transmission existed and had killed and infected more than two hundred people in China. By January 23, Wuhan was under complete quarantine. On February 2, global air travel became restricted in the United States and other nations, including Australia, Germany, Italy, and New Zealand. By five o'clock that day, US citizens who had left China would face a two-week home-based quarantine if they had been in the Hubei province of China.

President Trump on February 3, 2020, declared that the United States was in a public health emergency, and immediately put in place a travel ban to and from China. The World Health Organization had declared a global health emergency just prior as more than 9,800 cases and 200 deaths had been confirmed worldwide. This was exactly two days before President Trump was officially acquitted by the US Senate from the impeachment proceedings.

The left immediately politicized President Trump's ban on travel to and from China. Chuck Schumer stood on the Senate floor and called the president's decision to stop travel racist and xenophobic. Pretty much the same thing the Democrats said about him when he restricted travel into the United States from Middle Eastern nations that did not have a vetting system for travel. The Democrats like to refer to it as "Trump's Muslim ban." Nancy Pelosi didn't waste any time jumping on the racist bandwagon either. Now, I would almost bet everything I have that they didn't truly disagree with the president at the time but were emotional (actually, extremely pissed off) that their recent impeachment stunt had utterly failed. That's my take on it.

Nancy got on live television and stated that people should not fear this virus—that it was nothing to be too concerned with. She then stated that she was disgusted with Trump's decision to ban travel to and from China, and even went as far as saying she encouraged everyone to go visit Chinatown in California, where she claimed to regularly visit and shop.

By February 25, the CDC announced that COVID-19 was heading toward pandemic status. Explaining what would justify this status, the director of the CDC said that COVID-19 had met two out of the three criteria: it was proving to be an illness that resulted in death and sustained person-to-person spread. Worldwide spread was the third criterium, but it was not there yet. However, in two months, as we all know, it was.

On March 13, President Trump declared the coronavirus a national emergency, which immediately unlocked billions of dollars in federal funding to fight the disease's spread. He also placed a second travel ban, on non-US citizens traveling to and from Europe. The president then ordered, under state oversight and control, to shut down businesses and schools for a period of time. This was done primarily until scientists could get more answers and education on this new virus, and to prevent its rapid spread across the globe.

March 26, the Senate passed the Coronavirus Aid, Relief, and Economic Security, or CARES, Act. This provided two trillion dollars in aid to hospitals, small businesses, and state and local governments, while including an elimination of the Medicare sequester from May through the remainder of the year. The next day, Trump signed the CARES act into law after the House of Representatives approved it. It was the largest economic recovery package in history. The bipartisan legislation provided direct payments to American taxpayers and expansions in unemployment insurance.

Also in March 2020, schools and universities were ordered to close nationwide in accordance with the president's advisory and as directed by state governors. That is another aspect that the left and media seemed to disregard—the fact that President Trump left these decisions up to the states to manage, as he should have.

I subbed the day that Governor DeWine of Ohio ordered schools and all businesses closed. I remember the date was March 13 because it happened to be Friday the 13th. Our high school was having a blood drive in our gymnasium that day. I went down during my conference period to check on how it was going. Half of the students who had previously signed up to give blood pulled out and refused to do so due to the fear of this new coronavirus. The Wood County blood-drive personnel were upset. I talked to one of the nurses, and she was pissed, stating that there hadn't even been a confirmed case in Wood County yet. That changed in the next couple of months—big-time. I went back to my classroom, thinking, *Well, that's up to the parents of these kids, period.*

During the final period of the day, student aids delivered letters to each classroom that the teachers had to read and pass out to the students to take home to their parents. The letter announced a probable chance that school would be closed soon for an undetermined period. These weren't just regular letters printed on regular copy paper, either. They were printed on nice, blue construction paper with a calligraphy-style font. I was impressed with the effort put into these letters for the parents of our community.

When I got home, I immediately turned on the news to see the latest status for our state. Governor DeWine was live on television, stating that school districts in the entire state of Ohio would be closed for an indefinite amount of time. School was officially closed for the remainder of the year. Senior classes would not have a graduation ceremony, nor a prom, etc. My son was a senior during this closure, and my wife and I asked him how the online system was working for him with his teachers. He admitted there was no contact whatsoever with any school staff, no more teaching, and no final exams either. They got the grades they had earned by mid-March, and that was it. Everyone just received a high school diploma in the mail.

While all schools and businesses were closed due to the virus, President Trump and his staff put together a group of scientists, primarily medical seniors and experts of disease control, along with lead senior chiefs of pharmaceutical companies to create an emergency response team to come up with a vaccine in a record period of time. The timeline would usually have been four to five years.

The last worldwide pandemic, during World War I, was the influenza of 1918. That H1N1 virus infected about five million people in the US and one-third of the world's population as a whole, killing at least fifty million worldwide and about 675,000 in the United States. To this day, scientists claim no country of origin has been pinpointed. I actually got the last major H1N1 virus, also known as the swine flu, while serving in Iraq during the summer of 2009, and I thought I was going to die from it. Yeah, I went to combat to die of the fucking flu—go figure.

As I'm writing this chapter, my wife and I have recently recovered from COVID-19. We were not that sick, to be honest with you. We had cold symptoms and of course lost our sense of taste and smell. That was the worst part of it because we like to eat spicy foods. One night my wife made tacos, and I was like, "Well, that's great, but too bad I can't taste them." We quarantined ourselves for ten days, per our county health department and work standards requirement. One thing I can say about the differences between the two diseases, after having both, is that COVID-19 takes about a week to start having symptoms, and H1N1 swine flu was within twenty-four hours. Swine flu was quick too, but for me it was more painful. I go into more details in my last book, *Wake Up, You're Having Another Nightmare*.

Getting back to President Trump's team, which he put Vice President Pence in charge of, the mission was named Operation Warp Speed, and its primary purpose was to produce a vaccine for this virus in less than a year. On top of producing vaccines, they were also charged with producing therapeutics and diagnostics. Immediately, Nancy Pelosi and the left criticized this effort, claiming that it was impossible to have a vaccine in a year or less. Why would the Speaker of the House tell the American people that it was going to be a failure? Because Donald Trump developed it—plain and simple. The mainstream media ran with it and viewed Operation Warp Speed as a probable failure.

CHAPTER 6

THE 2020 ELECTION: NEVER LET A GOOD CRISIS GO TO WASTE

This chapter coincides directly with the last. I rolled the COVID-19 crisis into the election year since the Democrats used it as Biden's main directive for his entire campaign plan—if that's what you want to call his sitting in his basement for six months. I'll get into the campaigning strategies of both parties in a little bit.

Let me take you back to the three or four years prior to the coronavirus and how I lost friends and family on Facebook. I already talked to you about my demise with my immediate family from Michigan, right? Let me get into some of the reasons my friendships dissolved on the big social media site.

Like I said earlier in the book, Republican supporters are going to be Republican supporters. The same goes for Democrat supporters, and that's the end of it. Going back and forth is useless when it comes to debating political party beliefs with one another. I have at least learned that in the fifteen years I have been on Facebook and the seventeen years I've been a registered GOP supporter. The only reason I initially got on Facebook was because when I first got my assignment as an Army ROTC instructor at Bowling Green State University in January 2006, Facebook was the newest internet connection for most, if not all, of the college students across this campus and most others across the country. Before then, there was only MySpace, which hardly exists anymore.

Getting on Facebook was a good way to connect with my cadets. As their instructor, I wanted to make sure they didn't fuck up their careers before they got into the military in the first place. I used Facebook to ensure that they were not acting inappropriately during their college experience—especially since our program at BGSU had some problems the previous year that led to dismissals. I looked at it as keeping an eye on them, not spying, because I couldn't care less who was dating who or how much they drank at the bars downtown. I wanted to be able to advise them of what not to post on this newly formed social media site. In the military, we are trained to not only train our subordinates in combat scenarios but to counsel and advise them as well. Anyway, that's how I got on the "big mighty Facebook." The funny part is that these days all the young kids cling to Instagram, TikTok, and Snapchat, and Facebook has turned into a site for us "old folks."

Again, I've been arguing and debating with others on Facebook about political decisions since Barrack Obama took office in 2009, even when I was still in the Army. For a leader in the military to criticize the commander in chief's decisions or policies is discouraged, but I did it anyway, since I knew I was going to retire the next year. What was the Army going to do, terminate my retirement paperwork?

Now, when I say criticize, I don't mean being disrespectful of him or the office he holds. That is not in my character. I would never call anyone a bad name or be disrespectful in any way, shape, or form. You can take that to the bank. However, those who I have argued with on Facebook would use these tactics, or friends who agreed with me would start dropping f-bombs and calling names. The next thing you knew, shit would get personal, as it did between me and my mother and other family members numerous times.

One thing I noticed during political debates on social media was that the person on the left always loved to cut and paste articles they believed would prove their points beyond a reasonable doubt. Fuck, there were times I thought I was in a court of law or at least debating a Harvard Law graduate. Of course, their articles would derive from CNN, MSNBC, or other liberal-progressive-leftist websites. The ones that really pissed me off and I eventually started ignoring were those who didn't have the ability to argue or debate respectfully but instead would answer me with memes or gifs. That is our younger generation, ladies and gentlemen.

Some debates I got into weren't even with friends. Instead, a stranger would jump into the argument I was having with a friend and try to belittle or intimidate me. I always gave it right back, but I did it without insulting them. I would argue the point with facts. That pissed them off even more, especially individuals with college degrees—those who saw themselves as the "elite members of society." The funny part is that when they got pissed they would eventually go after my education level, even though they knew nothing about me. They assumed that I was an uneducated "redneck" because I was arguing on behalf of President Trump's accomplishments. I would keep quiet for a while but then drop the bomb on them that I have a graduate degree, which is higher than the education of some who attempted to belittle my intelligence.

The best of all was when a snobby leftist would try to play the race card on me, thinking I am a white racist because I am a Trump supporter. When I broke it to them that I am half Mexican and come from a racially mixed family, that would piss them off badly enough to end the argument. Think about it: when you cannot tear a Trump supporter's race or education level down, what else do you have to throw at us? It's the same concept that drives the left's narrative away from the subject of racism when there are Black, Hispanic, Asian, or, God forbid, homosexual conservative Trump supporters.

The fact of the matter is this: My wife and I are Republican supporters, but just because I never agreed with any of Barrack Obama's policies or decisions—except of course his decision to approve the Osama Bin Laden raid—doesn't mean we didn't respect his position as president of the United States. The same when it came to Vice President Biden. You should always respect the office they hold, no matter what political party they belong to. But the press and the Democrats took disrespect of the office to a level this country had never seen prior to Trump's time in office. That's a fact.

To this day, my wife and I display my retirement certificate from the US Army with President Obama's signature in our home office where we display all our military plaques that she and I both earned from our time in service. Furthermore, we also proudly display a picture of my wife with Vice President Biden when he came to visit the facility she has been managing for the last seven years or so. One of the newest rail facilities in our country, the CSX Intermodal Terminal of Northwest Ohio was built with state-of-the-art cranes and computer systems, and began logistical operations in December 2010. Jessica was one of the original employees hired there, and she remains there to this day as one of the top four managers responsible for running its operations. So, she has a professional picture standing with now President Biden when he visited the facility back in 2013 or 2014. Again, we display it proudly because of the office he held.

My wife, Jessica Aguinaga, with the now forty-sixth president of the United States, President Joe Biden.

By the early weeks of summer 2020, cases of illness and death increased across the United States. New York state and California became the hardest hit. Hospital space for these patients was running out within the most populated cities, such as New York City, Los Angeles, and Seattle. Not just that, but more medical professionals were testing positive for COVID-19 themselves.

Trump's medical team pushed for social distancing of six feet, washing hands regularly, and wearing masks in public. Restaurants opening at a minimal capacity in certain states were already making it mandatory to wear a mask. In Ohio, we had to wear a mask and still do as of writing this; once we were seated, the mask could come off. If you got up for any reason, like to use the restrooms, the mask went back on. The owners were simply happy to have costumers back after the weeks of shutdown that spring. As you are already aware, disinfecting surfaces, doorknobs, etc., became the norm as well. My wife and I, even after having the virus ourselves, still disinfect regularly to this day.

Another major problem was that hospitals didn't have enough ventilators for their severe patients. Hospitals across the nation began exchanging ventilators to increase the number available in states that were the hardest hit, such as Washington state, New York, and California. Major manufacturing companies like General Motors, Chrysler, and Ford began producing ventilator systems at a rapid rate. They manufactured so many ventilators for our nation that the US began providing them to other struggling nations. I was impressed by how fast these machines were produced and the entrepreneurship that other companies displayed in producing masks and hand sanitizers in bulk. Our country seemed to be coming together and helping one another early last April and May.

With hospitals overwhelmed with COVID-19 patients, President Trump ordered military medical response teams to get involved. The US Army immediately sent active duty field hospitals and massive amounts of military medical personnel to cities like New York and Los Angeles. A battalion of Army and Marine medical personnel can put together a field hospital and have it fully operational within twenty-four to forty-eight hours. I've seen it done. They will work around the clock with no rest until it is complete. True professionals, ladies and gentlemen. Trump also ordered two massive Navy medical ships to the ports of New York City and Los Angeles. I'll be honest with you; I didn't even know the Navy had medical ships like this. I mean, these were literally floating major hospitals. Governors Cuomo (D) from New York and Newson (D) from California thanked President Trump publicly and on television for all he had done to assist them during this crisis.

With this medical crisis ongoing and increasing throughout the United States, another emergency-level activity was about to get underway. In Minneapolis, on the afternoon of May 26, 2020, a police officer named Derek Chauvin killed George Floyd. Mr. Floyd was a forty-six-year-old African American man. Officer Chauvin knelt on Floyd's neck for nearly eight minutes as three other officers stood by and allowed this to happen. Not only did they allow this murder to take place, they also prevented local bystanders from attempting to stop it. All four of these Minneapolis police officers were later arrested for the murder of Mr. Floyd. Other charges included police brutality and lack of police accountability. President Trump immediately announced his disgust and condemned the murder of Mr. Floyd. He also tasked the FBI to oversee this investigation.

That evening in Minneapolis, protests began. Word of this horrific murder quickly got around; everything was caught on camera as it occurred. The protests soon turned into riots throughout the country, including in Seattle, Portland, Los Angeles, Oakland, Detroit, Chicago, New York, and Atlanta. The rioting, led by angry mobs of pissed-off members of Black Lives Matter, or BLM, and so-called Antifa, or the anti-fascism movement, stormed across the nation.

This rioting has continued for so long that the narrative of Mr. Floyd's death isn't even being talked about anymore. BLM and Antifa turned it into an anti-American movement. I would bet you that half of them, almost a year later, couldn't even tell you who George Floyd was. As if it wasn't bad enough with the pandemic closing local businesses in these cities, these rioters—or, as I like to refer them, domestic terrorists—destroyed and burned businesses, and looted property and items from them, just as some of these business owners were trying to get back on their feet. This shit was happening on a nightly basis. Sure, free speech protesting is fine; that was what was occurring during daylight. As soon as the sun went down, all hell broke loose. This was 2020 in America. While hundreds of thousands of people in our country died from the pandemic, others were attacked on our city streets and businesses were destroyed and burned to the ground.

Oh yeah, did I mention that a presidential election was coming up while all of this was happening? While Trump tried to get America back to work, get our economy back, and get our kids back into school, he also told these blue-state governors and mayors to get control of these riots, or he would. He told them that if they could not get control of their cities, he would send federal law enforcement and military troops. The left of course attacked him for trying to turn US cities into war zones—which at that point they pretty much already were. He did send troops and US marshals into Portland and Seattle when federal buildings came under attack and federally protected monuments were being torn down by these mobs. Once these troops and marshals moved into these cities, shit began to calm the fuck down.

Never let a good crisis go to waste, right? Well, Democrats across the country and especially in Washington, DC, sure weren't. DC was a hot mess too. Rioters were even threatening to go over the fence and storm the White House. When Dan Bongino got word of this threat by Antifa, he got on *Fox and Friends* the next morning and practically begged them not to do it. He begged them out of fear not for the president and his staff but rather for the lives of the protestors themselves. As a former Secret Service agent for President Bush and Obama, he went live on television and told them that if they attempted to storm the White House, it would not turn out pretty for them. He was very vocal, as he always is, and pleaded with them to not even try it; it would be a bloodbath with all the security on the grounds of the White House that people really aren't aware of.

The left didn't hesitate to blame the pandemic and the riots on Trump, getting in front of the cameras, as they always love to do, to convince the American people at home that all of this catastrophe happened on Donald Trump's watch. I mean, it technically did, but state-elected officials are responsible for policing their own cities, and it wasn't happening. As I'm writing this, it still isn't happening in some cities. That's why I believe the days of Governors Cuomo, Newsom, and the mayors of Seattle and Portland are seriously numbered.

During the riots, Joe Biden was the Democrat primary candidate going against the incumbent president. He never condemned any of this anarchy until his poll numbers started to drop that September before the election. Hell, he pretty much never left the basement of his home the entire summer leading up to election day. He might have left once or twice but mainly stayed in the state of Delaware while he was supposedly on the "campaign trail." At the same time, Trump was pulling in crowds of thirty to forty-thousand people at every single one of his numerous, back-to-back rallies—in blue states, too. Joe Biden couldn't fill up a high school gymnasium.

The left's hatred for this man became more evident to the American people, and not just those who watch Fox News. When Donald Trump gave his final State of the Union speech, at the end, the Speaker of the House ripped it up in front of the entire Congress and the American people. You also had the new member of the so-called "squad," representative from Michigan Rashida Tlaib, get up during the speech and actually storm out of the chamber. Yeah, a real class act. Remember her celebration after she won the seat for the thirteenth district of Michigan? She said, "We're gonna impeach the motherfucker!" That was live on television too, and in front of her child. Could you imagine if a newly elected Republican congressman or woman had said that about Barrack Obama? I swear, they wouldn't be allowed to step one foot on Capitol Hill. When she said it, the left and the media applauded her.

Yeah, so our Congress has six members of the "squad" working in the US legislative branch of our government—six people who hate our country, everything it stands for, and everything it was founded on. I think that night at the State of the Union, Nancy Pelosi and the rest of the Democrats were pissed off that he was giving this speech at all. They thought he would bow out because of the impeachment, but he said fuck no. He never cowered to any of those crooked career politicians, and they hated him even more for it.

Okay, getting back to the campaigns. I'm not going to get into the Democratic primary race, because the candidates all had the same message: "I hate Donald Trump and I'm the one to defeat him." Otherwise, it was all about raising our taxes, giving free college tuition, stopping or even tearing down the wall, and providing free health care for "undocumented immigrants"—a.k.a. illegal aliens or illegal immigrants. I prefer to call them what they are, criminals, for entering our nation illegally in the first place, which is a crime. The Democratic candidates had no policies that would benefit the American people, especially the middle-class taxpayer.

So, by late summer 2020, it was down to former vice president Biden and President Trump. There was absolutely zero comparison between their campaign strategies. Trump went out and campaigned in different states, while the DNC kept Biden out of the public eye, except for giving small virtual speeches straight off a teleprompter. They had to do this because, as we all know, and I truly mean this with the utmost respect for the man, he couldn't put two complete sentences together. He would lose his train of thought in the middle of a sentence, and as our current president, he still does. I'm not making fun of his memory loss, because we're all going to be there someday, but I'm also not planning on running for president of the United States at age seventy-eight. When I was in high school, the left used to give

President Reagan a ton of shit for running for a second term because of his age. Hell, he was only seventy-one or seventy-two at the time.

Biden's entire campaign was that the economy was bad and Trump wasn't doing enough to fight the pandemic. He campaigned on getting as many vaccines out to people as possible by the following spring, giving the state officials everything they needed as far as medical and protective equipment, and getting our country back to work. My response was, "Oh, you mean everything that President Trump has done and is continuing to do now?" Give me a break. I repeatedly told my wife there was no way on God's green earth that this guy had any chance against Trump—and he didn't, but I'll get into that in a little while.

How soon all the Democrats "forgot" about the best economy our nation had ever seen going into 2020 before the pandemic, the defeat of ISIS, the rebuilding of our military, including a new branch, illegal immigration declining in record numbers, de-escalation with North Korea, and most of all, taking China down economically in order for the United States to get a fair trade deal with their regime. Yeah, they forgot all about those accomplishments, and I could go on, but, as I stated, that would be a complete book on its own.

So, while I'm on the subject of China, let me go back to the theory I briefly talked about earlier. You have to go back to the end of 2019. China's economy was at its worse in many years, maybe even as far back as when Mao Zedong took over in October 1949 and declared the creation of the People's Republic of China. President Trump was crippling their economy and strangling them on tariffs because they continued to stall on the second half of our trade negotiations. The funny part is that the United Nations still referred to them as a "developing nation." Are you kidding me—a developing nation? I don't know about your houses, but I can tell you that the majority of the stuff in mine, including clothing, televisions, other appliances, and furniture, all have a little tag on them that say *Made in China*. They are not "developing"; they are developed like a motherfucker.

Their goal for decades has been to become the global economic and military superpower, and to take that title away from the United States once and for all.

To make a long story short, we had them on their knees economically by the end of 2019. At the same time, a mysterious new virus allegedly developed in a wet market in Wuhan. Wet markets are disgusting and dirty with filth from live animals and rodents. I saw a couple of them when I was stationed in South Korea. I will not even try to describe the smell. So, it seemed possible, and the initial report from the World Health Organization was that the COVID-19 virus derived from this particular market in Wuhan. Recently it has been confirmed that the World Health Organization is investigating and questioning personnel from a scientific lab in Wuhan that has long worked with bat viruses. President Trump and his administration repeatedly highlighted the lab over concerns that the virus emerged from an accident there.

In January 2021, Secretary of State Mike Pompeo said new intelligence confirmed that the virus originated from this institution. Of course, the Chinese Communist Party will still deny it. Remember what they said when the virus was originally confirmed as a pandemic last year? Chinese officials made the false charge that American soldiers visiting the marketplace were responsible for the massive spread. Yeah right, because US soldiers tend to visit China and shop at disgusting wet markets. Um, no. Furthermore, US intelligence agencies have been monitoring this facility since it was reported that scientists were experimenting with different coronaviruses, possibly in order to develop a biological weapon for the Chinese regime.

Trust me when I say that I am not a conspiracy theorist, but hear me out on this one. Why wouldn't China allow this virus to infect the world, and especially the United States? Trump was heading for a win on our economy by the end of 2019, and they needed to disrupt this. They knew that if there was a pandemic and a medical crisis in the United States, President Trump's opponents would blame him for it, as they did. Trump's opponent in a presidential election would use a pandemic as a political tool against him. And China knew all this would happen if there were massive deaths in the US—especially during an election year.

You see, the big picture for China was that they needed Donald Trump out of office or their economy would continue on a path of sure collapse, not only because of the tariffs but also because of his strong immigration policies. China for many years had a large drug trade—mainly the lethal narcotic fentanyl, responsible for killing thousands of Americans every year—with the Mexican drug cartels moving it across the US/Mexican border. This trade was worth billions of dollars a year. With President Trump's wall and strong border policies and restrictions, China was losing those billions. Therefore, him being put out of office was as much a necessity for China as it was for the Democrats in Congress.

Going back to the 2020 election, the Dems and mainstream media were putting the blame of almost 350,000 deaths directly on the shoulders of Donald Trump. They continuously accused him of "not doing enough in a time of crisis." Seriously? The CDC initially announced that the United States could be looking at two and a half to three million deaths by the end of 2020. Instead, President Trump took charge immediately, closing down our borders to travelers from China and Europe—which, again, he was criticized for by the Dems and the news—and holding a White House press briefing with his medical team every single day for the first six weeks, and I mean every day. Some days it lasted up to two hours. He was also routinely praised by state governors for his expedience in pushing companies to make equipment and providing military medical teams. I guess the Dems forgot all about that. They believe that if you push a narrative long enough, people will start believing you, and the narrative grew the closer we got to the November elections.

What really pissed them off was that scientists and pharmaceutical companies confirmed that at least two vaccines had already been proven during human trials to be 95 percent effective at fighting off the virus, and that they would be out before the end of the year. This would be a world record of speed in creating a vaccine. Of course, those on the left were saying to the news cameras that they would be reluctant to take it because it had been developed under Donald Trump's watch. Even Biden and Kamala Harris said they would take it if the scientists advised them to, but not if Donald Trump did—as if President Trump, not scientists and the Food and Drug Administration, were creating and approving the vaccine, respectively.

When one of the president's personal doctors advised that the use of hydroxychloroquine with zinc could be a possible drug to combat COVID symptoms, the media immediately attacked Trump for suggesting it. Why? Because the suggestion came from President Trump's mouth. Hydroxychloroquine is a primary drug treatment for malaria and lupus. When President Trump was under treatment for the disease, he was given hydroxychloroquine. Today, as I write this portion of this book, it is being proven that this drug is effective in helping to treat patients with severe COVID. Now that President Trump is out of office, I guess it's okay for the media and "Big Tech" to allow the reporting of the positive effect of this drug.

I could not wait for November 3 to get here and all of this to be over; I and almost seventy-five million other Americans thought that Trump's second term was a foregone conclusion, but I'll get into that a little later.

Okay, enough about COVID-19 and the riots. You already know that 2020 was the worst. Let's move on to the election itself.

So, states were pushing voters to use a mail-in ballot back during the summer. Their reasoning was that it was too dangerous, especially for the elderly and those with medical conditions, to go out and vote in person. Now, as I said in my opening chapter, these were not absentee ballots that have to be requested. They were actually mailed to you by the counties. My wife and I received two in the mail even though we never requested them. We opened them up and, no kidding, there was no identity or signature verification required. I literally could have put false names and scribbled a signature on it, and they would have been counted as votes.

Of course, I did no such thing. Instead, we tore them up and threw them in the trash. Like I said, I understand absentee ballots and their processing. The voter must request the ballot either through regular mail or email, with a verified signature and a copy of a driver's license or other form of picture ID to verify your home of record. Once that is sent in, then your state of record will mail you a ballot, but your signature will be verified and matched with the request form you sent in prior. It is a very easy process. Again, I think I voted absentee at least three times in my twenty years in the Army and never had an issue. But that summer we got this bullshit in the mail that was never requested in the first place. Something was definitely not right about it.

This new mail-in-ballot system due to the coronavirus was bound to fail as far as proper accountability in many states. Particularly in blue states. I and over seventy-four million Trump supporters believed that then and still do to this day. Of course, Republican senators and congressmen, along with President Trump, warned that this was going to be a complete debacle, and that this was the Democrats' "hail Mary pass" during the final seconds of the game. The Democrats knew that with a vaccine on the way and President Trump's record, along with Biden's campaign being the weakest in our history, this was their only hope of beating him. They knew they weren't going to beat him at the ballot box. I mean, for God's sake, Donald Trump was drawing forty thousand plus out in the cold in Grand Rapids, Michigan, one of the bluest areas in that state. Joe Biden couldn't fill a town hall.

When Biden did press briefings, there were circles on the floor for each reporter, and his campaign managers would only select "their" news networks to ask the questions. Biden was not allowed to call on Fox News's Peter Doocy because Biden's staff knew he would get tough questions. They only wanted him to receive easy questions on what he thought about Trump doing this or Trump doing that. At one town hall, his team had already selected people to ask questions and knew what questions they were going to ask him; he was caught reading his answers from a teleprompter. The bottom line is that his campaign managers had him away from the cameras, people, and especially the media as much as possible during the 2020 campaign.

My flagpole in front of my house for approximately the entire year of 2020

My wife and I went to our county courthouse to vote. Yeah, we went early, but we did it in person, and our county had it figured out. As a matter of fact, Ohio as a whole had it figured out. As did the heavily populated states of Florida and Texas. We entered the courthouse and were immediately met by a police officer who checked our temperatures and then told us to proceed to the line. Of course, we were in masks. They had tape on the floor for the line that was spaced out accordingly. When we got to the front desk, we showed them our driver's licenses, and they scanned them and told us to grab a ballot card and proceed to two open ballot-computer booths. We were in and out of there in about seven minutes total. It was way too easy. Not only did we vote in person, but our two children, who are adults now, voted for their first time. We also talked a family we are friends with into taking their whole family over to vote, and they did for their first time too. So, about ten of us voted for Trump. Thousands of other families did the same thing across the country, getting other people to the voting booths for their first time. Actually, I should say over eleven million more people. That's how many more popular votes he received than the 2016 election.

CHAPTER 7

2020 ELECTION RESULTS: ALMOST 75 MILLION SKEPTICAL AMERICAN VOTERS

W hen I went to bed on November 3, 2020, President Trump was winning the election by a landslide. Of course, he had already won the majority of the red states. I believe the first state confirmed by the media was Kentucky. The only red state still in question—and which remained in question for days after the election—was Georgia. How the hell was Georgia not called on election night? I wasn't too worried about it and went to bed around eleven that evening, pretty confident that President Trump was going to win reelection easily. The counts even in the swing states such as Michigan, Pennsylvania, Wisconsin, and Arizona had him winning just prior to midnight of election night.

I woke up around 5:30 the next morning to find out that they were still counting votes in these swing states I just mentioned. They were still counting votes in the red state of Georgia. I immediately knew what it was all about. "I guarantee this shit is about the mail-in ballots," I told myself. But how could this be? Were there that many mail-in ballots delivered to these state voting sites? Or was it like the president predicted as far back as July? Other Republicans predicted the same outcome of a mail-in voting system. Jim Jordan, Lindsey Graham, Devin Nunes, and so on warned the American people that this was a threat to this election, and rife with the potential for voter fraud. Especially in swing states like Michigan, Wisconsin, and Pennsylvania—the states that cost Hillary Clinton the previous presidential election. As you are well aware, the entire country and the world patiently waited for the results from these states for days. When the results did come out on television, the mainstream media announced that Joe Biden had won the election. They claimed that he won the popular vote with over eighty-one million votes. As for Donald Trump, they claimed that he lost with a little over seventy-four million.

You are not going to convince me or the other seventy-four to seventy-five million who voted for President Trump that Joe Biden honestly received over eighty-one million votes. That would mean he received more votes than Barrack Obama and more votes than Hillary Clinton. No sir, I'm not buying it. If he had run an excellent campaign and pulled in tens of thousands of people like Trump did consistently, then I would believe that he received more votes than any presidential candidate in American history. But I do not, and after talking to a Democrat supporter, I believe many Democrats do not believe it either. What does it matter though, right? At the end of the day, Trump lost, and that's all they needed to hear.

Days after the media announced that Biden had won the election, President Trump refused to concede the results—rightfully. Instead, his legal team, which had already been prepared, led by Rudy Giuliani, immediately began their investigations into the swing states Arizona, Michigan, Wisconsin, Pennsylvania, and now Georgia. People working in some of those states' county voting centers were already reporting mail-in-ballot mishandlings.

We all remember the whole voter fraud scandal quite well. The mainstream media continued to tell their viewers that there was no evidence of voter fraud, when there was. The problem was that after hundreds of sworn affidavits and witnesses from these voting centers attesting to fraud, no federal judge wanted to touch any of the cases. After watching this process happen every day on the news, I learned that no judge wants to get involved with election-result disputes because it is political. If they decide a case for one side over the other in an election dispute, then they appear biased—especially when it came to the Supreme Court's decision to dismiss the lawsuit Texas presented against those specific states. Senator Ted Cruz from Texas was going to present the evidence of mass voter fraud to the Supreme Court. However, they dismissed it without hearing the case. The vote was seven to two with Judge Clarence Thomas wanting to hear the case. But, like I said, they didn't want to look biased towards Trump, especially the three justices he had appointed. Some looked at it like a slap in the face to the president, who fought for those three, especially Justice Kavanaugh. If they had heard the case and overturned those states' election results, the Democrats and the media would have lost their minds, and we all know that. So, that was that.

At that point, Senator Cruz led a movement among other Republican senators to debate the outcome and put a vote on the Senate floor to revoke those states' electoral votes when they were to confirm on January 6. It was a long shot, but it was also a last hope to overturn the election results through the legislative branch. The most frustrating part was that it wasn't even the states in their entirety that had issues; the alleged voter fraud occurred in only five major cities: Detroit, Milwaukee, Atlanta, Philadelphia, and Pittsburg.

On January 6, 2021, just a couple weeks before President-Elect Biden's inauguration, President Trump held his final rally in DC, with the White House in the background of the stage. I watched his speech live on the news. Thousands upon thousands of people attended from across the nation. It was a typical Trump rally speech that motivated and inspired his base with hope. Really, it was no different from the numerous rallies he'd had for the past five years, starting with his first campaign. I was lying on my couch watching it and fell asleep. When I woke up two hours later, I sat up quickly, and then stood in disbelief at what I was watching live on television—a riot of Trump supporters storming the Capitol Building. I got a sick feeling in my stomach as I watched. I yelled at the television, telling them to stop and go home. I knew exactly the outcome of this. There were going to be injuries and deaths, and they were going to go after Trump for it. "They" meaning Nancy Pelosi and Chuck Schumer.

The riot on Capitol Hill that day resulted in five deaths and many others injured. President Trump came out with a prerecorded video that aired on all news networks, telling the rioters to stop and go home peacefully. He said that it was over. Some would argue that he waited too long. The next day, he gave a speech of unity to our country. He condemned the rioters that stormed the Capitol and said that they were going to be prosecuted under the maximum extent of the law. He then said again that it was over, and he assured the American people that there would be a peaceful transition between administrations for the good of our nation.

The same day, Nancy Pelosi went to the cameras once again and threatened a second impeachment of President Trump for inciting the riot. At that point, I felt compelled to rewatch his speech in order to determine whether he incited that situation to happen. I watched it twice on YouTube, and I did not hear any rhetoric, as the left are accusing him of, that could be seen as inciting a riot. Instead, I heard him applauding the senators who were going to fight for overturning the electoral results from those few states with alleged voter fraud. He then said, "We are going to march down to our Capitol and cheer for those senators, and we are going to do it peacefully and patriotically."

Never once did he show any inclination for violence whatsoever. Had he done so, I would have stopped writing this, because I had the first couple of pages completed by the time that incident happened. I told my wife that I needed to see his speech at least two more times to ensure he never said anything about violence or breaking the law, which I knew he wouldn't, and he didn't. Too bad Mitch McConnell didn't watch it twice; instead he turned his back on Trump immediately and accused him of inciting the rioting. Again, another career DC politician. That's what they do best. They're experts at pointing their fingers at others to maintain their political status. What I believe, and many others do too, is that he turned his back on Trump because he blamed Trump for losing Georgia's two Senate seats, which gave the Democrats the majority in the Senate and relegated McConnell to the status of minority leader.

What pissed me off the most about what Pelosi and Schumer were doing, other than threatening impeachment again, was that they tried to lump all Trump supporters together with regards to this rioting incident. No, those people who stormed the Capitol should and are being punished and sent to jail. There are bad apples in every crowd, but do not lump me or the other over seventy-four million Americans who voted for our president in the same category as those individuals. Where were these Democrat leaders all summer while Antifa and BLM were burning down cities and rioting across the country? You didn't hear a damn word about it from any of them.

As a matter of fact, the left and the media continued to push a false narrative that the Capitol police officer who died was killed by a Trump supporter. This story of a rioter bashing the police officer in the head with a fire extinguisher was run for over forty-eight hours on all mainstream media. The police officer was proven to have died the next day from natural causes—of a stroke. There was no "fire-extinguisher incident" at all. CNN, MSNBC, ABC, etc., etc., never retracted their story after the autopsy report was made public. There was also no discussion of the unarmed female Trump supporter who was shot to death inside the Capitol. She was an Air Force veteran and a Trump supporter, so you didn't hear much about that from the fake-news networks either.

Anyway, that evening after everything calmed down on Capitol Hill, the Senate continued with their confirmation of electoral votes from each state. The vice president of the United States is traditionally responsible for certifying and calling off each state's results. President Trump did tweet out that VP Pence had the power to overturn and deny certain states on terms of voting fraud. He did not have that power. I believe his presence in the Senate is simply in accordance with a long tradition from the Constitution that the vice president will announce the certification. That evening Joe Biden officially became the next president-elect of the United States.

Nancy Pelosi kept her promise and continued to prove her hatred for Donald Trump. On January 13, 2021, the House of Representatives adopted one article of impeachment against Trump, which was incitement of insurrection. They did it in a matter of hours. No hearings, no defense witness, or witnesses at all for that matter— just a quick vote with the majority held by the Democrats. The same thing our Founding Fathers warned could happen if a majority-led party wanted to oust a sitting president. Thank God they created the second legislative branch. A few Republican representatives voted for impeachment as well, such as Elizabeth Cheney, who was leading the march on the Republican side of the aisle. Her career is over.

As I edit this portion of the book, she has just been dismissed from her House committee position by the Republican representatives. Therefore, she is surely done—at least in the "swamp." People are going to have to come to terms with the fact that the old ways of the Republican Party are over. The days of the Bushes, Cheneys, and Romney are over as well. Because of President Trump's strong "America first" policies and leadership, he remains the leader of the Republican Party. Since being voted out of her position in the House, Liz Cheney has gone on almost every cable news program to bash President Trump. She also continues to push the false narrative that he incited a riot at the US Capitol on January 6, 2021.

The votes in the House were in favor of impeachment, 232 to 197. Immediately after, Pelosi gave Vice President Pence an ultimatum to invoke section four of the twenty-fifth amendment to assume the role of acting president within twenty-four hours or the House would proceed with impeachment proceedings. Pence stated that he would not do so in a letter to Pelosi the following day, arguing that such an action would not be in the best interest of our nation or consistent with our Constitution. Shit, when has Nancy Pelosi ever cared about following the Constitution, right?

The Senate would not be back in session until 1 p.m. on January 20 to even conduct a Senate trial for the impeachment proceedings. By then, President Trump would be a civilian. Now, that would be against the Constitution. Remember, an impeachment is a political proceeding to remove an elected official, not a criminal court. The legislative branch of government cannot formally impeach a civilian citizen. But they damn sure went through with a Senate trial on February 9. Yeah, thanks to Mitch McConnell, they went through with an impeachment trial of a civilian.

Shortly after the Senate officially confirmed Joe Biden as the next president-elect, Twitter suspended President Trump's account. Soon Facebook fell in line and suspended him too. The conservative version of Twitter, Parler, lost their contract with Amazon. Parler attempted to sue the tech giant for breaching their contract, but a US district judge from Seattle dismissed the case. This started a domino effect with these Big Tech companies out of Silicon Valley removing the conservative voice, and fast. Some protested that the companies were breaching conservatives' first amendment rights, but those on the left argued that these companies had the right to suspend those with "hate speech," and furthermore had the right to do so because they were private companies. True, but this is 2021, and most communications, entertainment, research, and shopping are done through Facebook, Twitter, Apple, Google, and Amazon. At least, they are for me. I'm typing this book on my Apple MacBook Pro, while researching events and dates through Google, while promoting my books on Facebook and Twitter. Does that make sense? These Big Tech companies play a major role in our lives. They also have global superiority.

Along with the unions, especially the teachers' unions, the railroad companies and technology companies have major influence and roles in our elections. How? It is simple. They donate millions of dollars to campaigns, especially Democratic politicians. "We helped get you elected, so now you owe us this piece of legislation." It is a tit-for-tat or this-for-that scenario. To hell with legislation that helps the everyday American household.

That's why Trump had to go. He would not bow down to these companies or special interest groups. He would negotiate with them because nobody knew the game better than Donald Trump, and he wanted to help out the American workers and create jobs. It was that simple. He was not political; he was in it for us, and he was a threat to the swamp's ability to maintain their wealth and power. I used to say all the time, "One of the fastest ways to become wealthy in this country is to get elected to the legislative branch of our government in Washington, DC." All you have to do to get there, which is considered the hard part, is convince constituents to vote for you, but you need a lot of money to get to that level. That's where these special interest groups and Big Tech companies come into play.

Getting back to this last election debacle. Trump did not entertain Nancy Pelosi or Chuck Schumer on this whole impeachment thing, just like he didn't during the first one before the pandemic hit. He didn't seem too worried about it either. Just like the first one, it continued to divide our country and piss off a lot of voters. But let's be honest with each other; deep down, Nancy and Chuck know damn well that Trump never incited any riot. They had one purpose and one purpose only: to ensure that Trump can never run for public office again. But that wasn't going to happen. Just like before, the Senate would never vote "guilty" for this article. Remember, they needed sixty-seven votes to remove someone from office.

But wait a minute, he was already out of office! This shit drives me crazy and continues to be mind-boggling for half of our country. I swear, writing this book is therapy for me.

On January 20, 2021, at approximately 8 a.m., President Trump and his beautiful wife, First Lady Melania Trump, left the White House for the last time (at least, for the next four years). They entered the Marine One helicopter for flight to Joint Base Andrews, where he and his entire family would fly on Air Force One down to Palm Beach, Florida, and on to his Mar a Lago estate. He gave one last speech when he arrived at Joint Base Andrews. I actually had tears in my eyes. I couldn't believe it was over. All those accomplishments—gone. Because I knew as soon as Biden was sworn into office as the forty-sixth president at noon, he would start signing executive orders to undo everything Trump achieved. I wake up four months after the election of 2020 and still cannot believe that this is a reality. I guess it's the same way everyone felt when Hillary lost, except you won't see me screaming up at the sky like her supports did. Nor will you see me protesting or rioting. No, writing this book is good enough for me.

President Trump said his farewell to the nation live on television, and assured that he would be back "in some sort of fashion in the future." My bet is that he will run again in 2024 because let's face it, he remains the leader of the Republican Party. He never did concede the election results, nor did he attend President Biden's inauguration. He was the fourth president in US history to not attend his successor's inauguration ceremony. There was John Adams in 1801, John Quincy Adams in 1829, Andrew Johnson in 1869, and now Donald Trump in 2021.

Within six hours after President Biden was sworn into office, Biden began signing executive orders to undo what the former president had accomplished. The first order was to immediately stop the Keystone/XL Pipeline production, which would kill over eleven thousand jobs. The second order was to immediately stop production of the southern border wall, which killed about another ten thousand jobs. Within the first six hours of being the president of the United States, President Biden put over twenty-one thousand union workers out of jobs.

Why close down production of the pipeline? It goes back to what I was telling you about corporate influence in political campaigns. Biden knows that system better than anyone in Washington, DC. The man has been there almost his entire adult life. He was elected as the youngest US Senator in history back in 1973. I am forty-nine years old, so that means I was one year old when he got to "the swamp."

Experts like Daniel Turner, the founder of the energy group Power the Future, claimed recently that closing construction of that pipeline had nothing to do with green energy or environmental safety. That's what "the swamp" Democrats have been selling to the American people for decades. Oil has been transferred from

Canada to the United States all along. The difference is that it used to be transported by rail. The new Keystone Pipeline would run the same product from Canada to Texas, and the rail corporations were pissed off at losing that business. So they poured millions into Biden's campaign. In return, Biden had to shut down that production, and that was the first thing he did after walking into the Oval Office. This for that, right? Green energy is a left-wing farce lasting for generations now. Steven Koonin, from the Obama administration's Department of Energy, recently admitted, "Science has been manipulated by the far left in order to scare the young voters in our country. They continue to push the climate change narrative."

When it came to the stoppage of wall production on our southern border, President Biden knew exactly what he was doing. What's the fastest way to turn the state of Texas into a blue state? Allow floods of illegal aliens to enter. Democrats would be guaranteed almost 100 percent of the vote. If the state of Texas turned blue, there would never be a Republican president in the White House again. Biden knows this. He's been in DC for almost fifty years. Within the same few days of him taking office, he also signed an executive order to stop the "Remain in Mexico" agreement for those claiming asylum from the countries they were fleeing. This order, and the end of wall construction, automatically meant there would be a massive flood of illegal aliens into the continental United States.

By March 2021, over 170,000 illegal aliens had come through our southern border. This is the highest number in over twenty years, if not longer. Border Patrol leaders say that the number will reach one million before the end of summer 2021. That number was documented and recorded by US Border Patrol from California, Arizona, New Mexico, and Texas. It is estimated that thousands more got through undetected due to gaps in the unfinished portions of the wall and lack of security on the border itself. This lack of security is because almost half of our Border Patrol agents must attend to and care for the thousands of children in detainment facilities along the southern border. Most of these unaccompanied children are being held for weeks at a time. The law says only seventy-two hours maximum. If President Trump held any child one hour over, he would be called a Nazi by the media. Under Biden, children are being held for a month and nothing is reported about it.

I won't get into the other twenty-five or thirty orders he signed in his first ten days in office. I don't think he even knows what the hell he's signing. The far-left progressives in the swamp just keep piling them up on his desk, and he signs them like Christmas cards. Just like Trump warned would happen. For those who hate President Trump and voted for Joe Biden in the hopes of having Trump out of the White House, there's an old saying—be careful what you wish for. What took President Trump four years to accomplish for our nation, Biden was able to undo in four short months.

One point I do want to hit is the status of our schools being reopened. As I write this chapter, President Biden's administration has been in office for over 130 days. One of his biggest points in his campaign against President Trump was the necessity of reopening our schools across our country, as President Trump had already been saying for the six months prior to the 2020 election.

Northwest Ohio, in particular the small villages such as our town of North Baltimore, figured out how to open our schools safely. As a substitute teacher at North Baltimore Middle/High School, I have witnessed it daily as our school district has been in full session since August 2020. At first, during the beginning of the fall semester in August and September, we had to separate our classes weekly. So, for example, on Mondays and Tuesdays we would have half of a class in the school. On Thursdays and Fridays, the second half would come in, and Wednesdays were dedicated to strictly online. Yes, the classrooms were pretty empty compared to the normal capacity, but the students were in the classrooms, not only learning the required curriculum but also maintaining social development by socializing with friends and peers—a requirement for human development at a young age. We all knew kids in school who were loners and didn't really associate with their classmates, but to have that status forced upon all students by teachers' unions was unheard of until this past year.

What do I mean by this statement? It's simple. Teachers' unions poured millions of dollars into Biden's campaign, as they do for every Democrat candidate at all levels of political empowerment, particularly states and cities. Now the power of the White House, House of Representatives, and the Senate too is at their beck and call. In other words, demand millions and billions of dollars of legislation passed, or threaten to keep the classrooms closed, right? I mean, that's what they're doing now as I write this. Their excuse again has a continuous motto: we demand federal aid from Washington, DC, in order to make our schools safe from COVID-19 or we'll keep our schools closed—pretty much all from Democratic-run states and cities. President Biden and Vice President Harris know this and are complying with these unions' demands. Again, they think that the American people are too naïve and stupid to realize what is going on with this situation.

So, this is how the school district where I work runs our safety precautions in order to keep our schools open. Like I said, classes were broken in half during the school week. This was the standard until around the beginning of October 2020, and then it was back on with full classrooms for all students, Monday through Friday, including all sports. How did our district figure it out? Because our superintendent, principals, and staff wanted to figure it out. First and foremost, all students and staff wear masks throughout the entire day, unless they are eating or drinking, primarily at lunchtime. The students are spaced out within the classrooms. Before every class, the teachers check the temperatures of every student entering their classrooms. If the student has a temperature of over a hundred, they are sent to the office for their parent or guardian to pick them up. In between classes, the teachers are required to sanitize each desk or sitting area.

During lunch, the students are spaced out at least six feet in the lunch line, with teachers assigned to monitor. Students must sit at a table of no more than four until the teacher announces what section can enter the line to get their food. Once they have their food, they can take off their masks in order to eat. If they get up from the table to throw their Styrofoam containers out, they must have their masks on. Teachers enforce the standards at all times. The students then sit back down at their tables until told to leave in sections back to their respective classrooms for their next assigned period.

So, the bottom line: Northwest Ohio has pretty much figured out how to keep our kids in school and keep them social with one another. Blue states and cities are having a problem making this happen because of teachers' unions demanding funding. Depression and even suicide rates have increased in today's youth due to seclusion. The teachers have their unions to fight for them to stay out of schools, and the students only have their parents to fight for them to remain in school. Again, never let a good crisis go to waste when it comes to the political realm.

The American Federation of Teachers, the second largest teachers' union in the United States, recently had meetings with the CDC on whether or not schools should be opened up in certain states (blue states). This particular union has been advocating to keep these schools closed—one-third of our nation's schools—at the time of writing this paragraph (May 2021). The CDC confirmed last fall semester, in 2020, that it was safe for children to go back to school, with the safety regulations being enforced. So why in May 2021 does the CDC need to meet with the second-largest teachers' union in the country? I'll tell you why; so that they can be coerced to publicly make statements that certain areas of the country need to keep their school districts closed— pretty much the entire West Coast and New York State. Teachers have been caught stating that conducting online education makes their lives easier . No shit! Sorry, get up, take a shower, get dressed in nice clothes, and go do your jobs educating children in the classrooms.

Speaking of what is being taught to our students in the past couple of months, critical race theory is being introduced in schools—not only in universities, which have been teaching this radical left propaganda for decades now, but in K through 12 as well. It is derived from the 1619 Project, which was introduced by writers from the *New York Times*. Their articles aimed to reframe the country's history by placing the consequences of slavery and the contributions of Black Americans at the very center of our country's national narrative. The project was first published in the *New York Times Magazine* in August 2019 for the four hundredth anniversary of the arrival of the first enslaved Africans in the English colony of Virginia.

This is basically the far left's interpretation of the "birth of the United States," rather than basing our nation's origin on our independence from British rule in 1776. It is complete indoctrination for our children, teaching guilt and prejudice due to the color of someone's skin—Marxism in action, or Communism 101. Rule number one: turn a nation's people against one another by using race and socioeconomic privilege in order to divide. The left has been doing it since the 1960s. Now they're introducing it in grade school. Change history and it becomes new history for the young, as communist governments have been known to do throughout history.

This movement has even been forced into our military now. Lieutenant Colonel Matthew Lohmeier, a commander in the newly formed US Space Force, wrote a book about how the military is pushing this Marxist mentality on our active duty service members. He went on a podcast to promote his new book. When the military found out about it, he was relieved of his duties of command. Now, what really upsets me with this narrative is that the far left has made their way into high-ranking-command cabinet members of the Biden administration. General Austin, the newly appointed secretary of defense, apparently turned into a politician after he retired from active duty. He was my brigade commander in the 82nd Airborne Division back in the late 1990s, so it bothers me that he is pushing this radical left agenda onto our military. What bothers me the most is that General Milley is following Austin's orders and pushing this ideology as well.

As a retired senior noncommissioned officer in the Army, I can tell you that it will fail in the ranks of our military. No soldier or noncommissioned or commissioned officer is going to buy into this crap or teach this radical left "garbage" to our soldiers. They will not follow the orders of the higher chains of command, such as division and brigade-level commanders, who politically push this agenda onto the battalion and company levels. I know I wouldn't teach it, nor would any of my subordinate leaders. This is going to cause a rift within the military. If that happens, our country is truly in trouble.

I recently watched an interview with an elderly Chinese woman who was around and remembered the communist revolutionary takeover of China. The communists used critical theory to divide their people as well, pitting the wealthy against the middle class and poor. She was on FOX News, warning against what would come with critical theory if the radical left gets their way.

Speaking of changing history, how about the way this Biden administration continues to deny that there is a current crisis on our southern border? Instead, they call it a "complicated situation" that is under control, and that it was an "inherited problem from the Trump administration." Again, a complete lie, because when Biden was sworn into office on January 20, the border problem was ended. By 2020, illegal crossings were down over 80 percent. The left has continued to push their own narrative for the past four months that Biden's been in office. I guess if you say it enough times and the mainstream media helps you push the narrative, eventually the citizens of a nation will believe it.

How about the high inflation and gas prices, or the East Coast's fuel crisis due to the Colonial Pipeline cyberattack by the Russians? Cars were lined up for hours to fill their gas tanks, and physical assaults broke out between citizens. Our country hasn't seen anything like this since the Carter administration. Actually, the Biden administration has already proven to be "Carter 2.0."

Don't even get me started on the new war in the Middle East between the Palestinians and Israel. Leaders of the terrorist group Hamas, which is funded, equipped, and completely supported by the Iranian regime, launched thousands of rockets into the cities of Jerusalem and Tel Aviv in the state of Israel in May 2021. As expected, Israel retaliated. For President Trump's time in office, it was virtually quiet in that region of the Gaza Strip. As a matter of fact, another of Trump's major accomplishments was the Abraham Accords peace deal he and Secretary Pompeo brokered between Israel and Arabic countries. The first countries to sign the agreement were the United Arab Emirates and, shortly after, Bahrain. Next was Sudan, and the fourth country was Morocco. This was historic—the first time in world history that Sunni Arab nations agreed to peace with Israel. The alliance was built to counter the lasting threat of the Iranian regime.

Okay, let me stop complaining about our current administration and get back to the core of this book.

The next few years seem certain to be a challenge for our country. As Mark Lavine told Fox News opinionated conservative host Sean Hannity not too long ago, "We are Americans, and we will work our way through what is to come. We have made it through hard times in the past, and we can do it again." He was basically reassuring the viewers to stay strong in the upcoming four years—and warning that it may be a bumpy ride.

I felt compelled to write this book because of everything that has happened within our country in the last four to five years, ever since President Trump came down that escalator in the summer of 2015. I wanted to explain in writing how this nation's divide has affected not only politics, law enforcement, and immigration, but also my life personally.

I am Nathan Aguinaga, a retired military service member, author, proud husband and father, and a Trump supporter. I am also a Middle America "deplorable," and a "loser who shops at Walmart." I "cling to my guns and religion" while the elites fly over my state of Ohio, as they travel to and from the East and West Coasts. I am also a US taxpayer, and have been since I was sixteen years old. I started working and paying taxes and into social security when I was in tenth grade and started working at Little Caesar's Pizza in my hometown of Lapeer, Michigan. I'll be fifty years old next year. Donald Trump is the first president in my lifetime that kept every promise he campaigned on, and then some. He is the first president in US history to ever be impeached by the House of Representatives twice. He will also go down in history as one of the best and strongest presidents our country has ever had.

He had a message to the people of the freest society this planet has ever seen—the United States: "Our human rights come from the grace of God, not from government." This is the overall belief of conservatism throughout the world.

The late Rush Limbaugh repeated this to the American people and the millions of us who used to listen to him daily for over thirty years on radio. One thing is for sure: we both knew that Donald J. Trump was going to win the 2016 GOP primary race and become the forty-fifth president of the United States.

After Rush died in February 2021 from stage four lung cancer, President Trump went on several Fox News shows to share his memories of the short friendship he had with the conservative radio talk show icon. Surprisingly, Trump admitted that he did not become friends with him until after Trump came down that escalator in summer 2015. President Trump would call him to check on his status during his battle with cancer, and they remained good friends until Rush's death. In 2020, at President Trump's final State of the Union Address to our nation, he awarded Rush Limbaugh with the Presidential Medal of Freedom—the highest civilian award that any American can receive.

Rush and President Trump became good friends during his presidency.

President Reagan once gave a warning to the American people back in 1961. He saw how the radical left could easily take our country in a direction that would mirror once prosperous nations such as Cuba and Venezuela. He said, "Freedom is never more than one generation away from extinction."

President Trump always had the utmost respect for and loyalty to President Reagan, and always spoke highly of him, not only during Trump's presidency but also before when he was a civilian businessman.

I heard a comment on *Fox & Friends* this morning that stuck with me and made a great deal of sense. Will Cain said, "Civilizations are difficult to build, but very easy to tear down." Is this happening now in the United States? Are we at risk of losing our freedoms and civilization as a whole? Are we at risk of losing our status as leader of the free world? I believe we are, and it scares me. I believe our country is being plagued by the radical far left's attempts to change our history and indoctrinate our children to believe our nation was built on "oppressors against the oppressed." The far left is pushing the narrative that white people are the oppressors and those of color are victims. Turn society against itself, and the government can more easily take control.

I'm not attempting to use scare tactics on you, ladies and gentlemen, trust me. Being in the military for twenty years, I have seen and lived in other countries where basic freedoms are taken away by their governments. I've been in countries where women are not allowed to drive a vehicle or even sit in the front passenger seat. I was stationed in Germany for two years, where the people had to pay 50 to

60 percent income tax to their government. In return, they were given welfare programs, such as rent-free apartments. As a young twenty-one-year-old, I thought, *Wow, that's a pretty great way of life—to have the government pay for your apartment.* Now, as a middle-aged adult, I realize it was socialized redistribution of wealth. There is no better country to live in than the United States of America.

President Trump once warned our nation, and the almost seventy-five million Americans who voted for him last November, with one of the most powerful statements I believe he ever made. He was at one of his 2020 campaign rallies. I can't remember what state he was in at the time, primarily because he sometimes traveled to three a day. Nobody could catch up and account for this man's energy level. He talked about the radical left's true agenda. He said, "They're not really after me; they're after you. I just happen to be in their way."

DISCLAIMER

am not sure that this is even a strong disclaimer, because what I
wrote about General Mark Milley is how I truly still feel. He was
an excellent commander during my time serving with and under
him. He had an excellent military career that any senior leader in the
military would desire to emulate and aspire to achieve. Under the
Trump administration, he was a top-notch military advisor to the
former president, especially during our nation's fight against ISIS
and other terrorist organizations. However, regarding the debacle of
the US's hasty withdrawal from Afghanistan, I have to say General
Milley should have not gone along with Biden's decision to leave the
way we did. At minimum, perhaps he should have resigned, because
I guarantee that he advised Biden to leave the 2,500 troops that
were there as a contingency against the Taliban and other terrorist
organizations. He definitely advised him to leave Bagram Air Base
open under the control of US forces.

Also, shortly after the withdrawal from Afghanistan, General
Milley was accused of undermining President Trump after the 2020
election by calling his Chinese counterpart to warn him that there
could be a possible attack from the United States. It was leaked to the

media that he had called him not once but twice due to his concerns that President Trump could become unstable because of his anger with the election results. Former President Trump stated that if General Milley had called General Li of China to warn him of a US strike, then that would be considered treason, which is legitimate. There will be upcoming congressional hearings on this matter soon, so we'll have to stand by and wait for the results.

In my honest opinion, General Milley should have retired from active duty once it was confirmed that Joe Biden would be the forty-sixth president of the United States. Unfortunately, once military officers accept the rank of general, appointed and approved on Capitol Hill, they become politicians, whether they want to or not. I actually have current friends that retired as full bird colonels in order to decline the rank of brigadier general. When I asked them why, they all had the same answer: "I refuse to become a politician." General Milley has proven this danger; he showed that he is willing to move to the left under the current Biden administration when he pushed the critical race theory into our military ranks.

I felt it necessary to add this at the end, due to me finishing and contracting this book prior to the current administration's problems and/or failures. Thank you all.

AFTERWORD

From Jessica Mary Aguinaga

T o give you a little background on me, other than being Nate's wife, I grew up in the same town as Lisa, who wrote the foreword. She described our upbringing perfectly. I happened to go to the same Catholic Church she did, and was able to avoid the one stoplight we had in town by taking Elm Street instead of Main Street when I drove to her house. Our high school taught the typical curriculum of our time, there was no internet, and we both were honored to be in our high school's Air Force Junior ROTC program and activities. One such activity was raising the flag for the Friday night football games during the national anthem, where everyone stood, took off their hats, and placed their hands over their hearts out of pride, not obligation.

The household I grew up in consisted of my older brother and me, one dog, one cat, and both parents. My mom was a homemaker and my dad was a steelworker in downtown Cleveland, and a proud Vietnam veteran. We went to church on Sundays. We ate a home-cooked dinner together every night while we talked about our days. We went camping in the Alleghenies for vacation, and once a year we got to visit the zoo. We were as apple pie, Norman Rockwell painting,

American flag flying proudly in the front yard as you could get, and I loved my upbringing.

I understand now that growing up the way I did is nearing extinction. It makes me nostalgic to think back on it, but I am happy to move forward in life with my family and society, with all the technology and differences in practices. I have paused with concern many times during my adulthood as I watch our government, though. I have witnessed many instances where our leaders bow down, literally, to foreign dignitaries at the expense of our national pride and sovereignty. I have watched the education system turn in a direction of not just liberalism but teaching our children that socialism may be better for our nation and that they should be so politically correct as to apologize if they do not fall under a minority demographic. The basic curriculum used now in many ways has omitted true, documented events and facts because they are no longer popular—as if learning about slavery and historical figures involved with it will encourage us to condone the practice instead of learning from it. Through the years it has felt like so much of what I loved about this country has rapidly slipped away. Then Donald Trump came down that escalator and announced his run for president.

During Trump's presidency I observed the United States move in the direction I longed for. We were securing our borders and showing strength to the world while being able to back off of military operations that led nowhere. I know people who unfortunately have passed by now but who could have really benefitted from Right to Try, not to mention the VA has been getting cleaned up, and Trump's push for a vaccine for COVID has saved millions. I personally felt the effect of the corporate tax cuts in my bonuses from work during the years Trump was in. He really did put America, and her people, first. About time someone did that again. I felt I could get on board with the direction his leadership was taking us, and I was enthusiastic about the 2020 election. I did my part and voted in person, and encouraged several friends and neighbors to get in and vote—people who haven't voted since Clinton.

I won't dwell on the end state of the election, but the bottom line was there was going to be a change in administration. I figured, *Fine, I'll get back to the polls in 2022 and 2024.* Meanwhile, I have to sit back and watch the rapidity with which the new administration has unraveled all the ground gained in Trump's term. Watching this train wreck happen, and hearing the liberal commentary and justification of these rash actions, I was reminded of something—a book I had to read as part of a typical high school curriculum, George Orwell's *Animal Farm.*

I have noticed the push for a socialist America that liberals have been peddling for years, but never before have so many in the Democratic Party, or media, been so blatant about it. Mix that with the endorsement for such an agenda from "Big Tech," and we have the beginning of a society that sounds like something you read about in dystopian fiction when they talk about how it all started. This is what made me think about *Animal Farm.* In the story, the concepts sounded good and fair at first, but as time went on, the characters found themselves governed in a far worse way then they were before. What they thought would be utopia and equality amongst all of the animals turned into the elite, who placed themselves on top, oppressing the other animals worse than ever; all those promises from the time when they were being recruited into this lifestyle after the rebellion were broken. Those in charge knew they would meet some resistance from those who remembered how it used to be, and they met it with persuasion and force if need be. But all you really have to do is put the changes in motion, wait for those who knew a different way of life to die off, and assimilate the upcoming generations to know only the world you staged. This made me want to read George Orwell's *1984.*

Orwell's *1984* has been terrifying to read because literally every concept the main character is talking about—how Big Brother runs their lives and society—has been presented in current affairs in one way or another. First off, it's crazy to think how perceptive he was on the use of technology for monitoring citizens' habits and actions. Orwell was almost a Nostradamus of his time, looking into this futuristic ability technology provides. The helicopter looking in the apartment windows to see what people are up to would be too easy with a drone. Then there's the TV with constant propaganda videos; today you can't sit anywhere in an airport without CNN repeating the same, and in *1984* the TV can see you too, in which case we are not far off.

Technology can make an authoritarian nation's people paranoid beyond our wildest imaginations. Numerous political parties of the past have wanted complete control of the people and even resorted to genocides for it, for example Rwanda in 1994, the Third Reich, Khmer Rouge, etc. Could you image if a Hitler-like roundup of society's "parasites" had the assistance of 23andMe, drones, Alexa, GPS, Google search histories, and databases? Instead of six million people who could not evade the storm and were murdered, double or triple it. I'm not trying to go down the road of a conspiracy theorist, but if you wait until it happens to try to prevent it, good luck.

We are in a delicate time, the beginning phases of a different, uncertain era. You should take pause when a government says they are taking away your jobs, but you can just find a new one, or they'll find a way to take care of you later, and then they don't. Ronald Regan said it best: "The nine most terrifying words in the English language are 'I'm from the government, and I'm here to help.'" You should take pause when a president of the United States is successfully censored, then banned by Big Tech corporations like Twitter and Facebook, which are supposed to be open forums for free speech.

Alexandria Ocasio-Cortez said, and I'm paraphrasing, that we need to rein in the media, saying that they shouldn't be able to spew disinformation. Of course, she's talking about what she thinks of as the correct information, in no quantitative measurement. If she and her likeminded people don't perceive it as truth, then it shouldn't be allowed to be said at all—rather than allowing people to hear information for themselves and decide what they believe to be true. No, don't give citizens the license for free thought; rather, have only one opinion approved and disseminated by your party. Hey, AOC, I have a great idea. Let's make a committee for information approval and call it the Ministry of Truth (Orwell, *1984*; the Ministry of Truth concerns itself with news, entertainment, education, and the fine arts).

Lastly, as a person who enjoys studying history, I find it sad how they want to erase it. A child will be hard pressed to find a statue or mention in schoolbooks of our Founding Fathers, Civil War generals, or other people who should have a place in history, whether their story was good, or bad, or both. On the theme of *1984*, society has only to tear down statues and get rid of written works before in a few generations it's as if it never happened. Orwell mentioned whoever controls the present controls the past, and I see how true this is currently. Once you "bring the past up to date," change history, and start working on changing the language and what is acceptable to say, then the whole climate of thought will be different, because there will be no thought as we know it today.

Sorry to rant, but there is a lot to think about involving the direction of our beautiful nation. I always have, and still do, think that the United States is the best nation on earth. I am only saying that from the experience of having traveled to multiple other nations during my time in service, and seeing the way other populations are governed and live. There is no freedom like the freedom we have as Americans. It gives me comfort in knowing that we are still holding on, and that so many feel the same way I do about this great land and our precious and delicate independence. This is why I thank President Donald J. Trump for working so hard to reestablish a strong America, and my husband for writing this book, which captures how so many of us "deplorables" are thinking and feeling right now.

—JESSICA MARY AGUINAGA
Terminal Operations Supervisor,
CSX Intermodal Terminals,
Northwest Ohio

ACKNOWLEDGMENTS

First and foremost, I want to give my condolences to those families that have lost their loved ones due to the coronavirus this past year. My wife and I sincerely send you our prayers. Thank you to President Donald Trump for what you have accomplished on behalf of us Americans during your entire presidency. You put us first above anything else in your life, especially above politics. Thanks to my wife, Jessica Aguinaga, whom I mention quite often throughout this book, including her thorough and awesome afterword that she put her wholehearted efforts into. Thanks to John Koehler and the great men and women of Koehler Books for continuing to support my writing and making the publishing process simple. Thank you to the Fox News Channel and all the voices—from the early mornings with *Fox & Friends* to well into the late nights—I have been watching for real, truthful news for the past fifteen years. Thank you to the late Rush Limbaugh and his family again, whom I dedicate this book to. You brought conservative input into the light for us all over thirty years ago. Most of all, I would like to thank all of you who have purchased and read my books throughout the past couple of years. I hope I was able to entertain you, as I try to keep my writing style simple and to the point—but most of all, real. God bless you all.

CPSIA information can be obtained
at www.ICGtesting.com
Printed in the USA
LVHW071713121021
700248LV00004B/148

9 781646 634927